The Physician-Computer Conundrum: Get Over It!

William F. Bria, II, M.D.
Richard L. Rydell, M.B.A.

HIMSS Mission

To lead change in the healthcare information and management systems field through knowledge sharing, advocacy, collaboration, innovation, and community affiliations.

Printed in the U.S.A.   5 4 3 2 1

Requests for permission to make copies of any part of this work should be sent to:

Permissions Editor
HIMSS
230 E. Ohio, Suite 500
Chicago, IL 60611-3269
nvitucci@himss.org

ISBN 0-9725371-3-9

For more information about HIMSS, please visit www.himss.org.

To my wife Lee, our sons Bill and James, and my sister Rosemarie.

— William F. Bria, II, M.D.

To my wife Cheryl; our children Wendy, Vicki, Libby, Rod, Jill, Erika and John; our grandchildren Richie, Emma, Anna, David, Claire, Harris, Kylie, Chase, Drew, Cheryl, Jacob, Andrew and Tanner; and in loving memory of Sandra.

— Richard L. Rydell, M.B.A.

Contents

About the Authors

William F. Bria, II, M.D., is Clinical Associate Professor of Internal Medicine and Medical Director of Clinical Information Systems at the University of Michigan School of Medicine in Ann Arbor. He is a member of the Pulmonary and Critical Division of the Department of Medicine and has a joint appointment in the Department of Medicine and the Medical Center Information Technology department. Dr. Bria is a Fellow in the American College of Chest Physicians and he is the Medical Co-Director of the Medical ICU and Asthma Airways program at the University of Michigan.

Dr. Bria has been a leader in Applied Medical Informatics for over 20 years. He has authored numerous articles and book chapters on informatics and co-authored the book, *The Physician-Computer Connection*.

Dr. Bria has been a consultant for the Institute of Medicine on the Computerized Patient Record and to the United States Congress relating to the application of information technology to the practice of medicine. He has lectured on medical informatics throughout the U.S. and around the world.

Dr. Bria is currently the president of Association of Medical Directors of Information Systems, was the past president of the

Medical Information Systems Physicians Association, and serves on the review boards of the *Journal of Healthcare Information Management* and *Healthcare Informatics*. He is currently engaged in research in applied medical informatics and asthma disease management.

Richard L. Rydell, M.B.A., is a Founder and Executive Director of the Association of Medical Directors of Information Systems (AMDIS). Mr. Rydell has a distinguished career as a healthcare executive, serving as a Senior Vice President and Chief Information Officer at Memorial Health Services, Long Beach; Stanford University Medical Center; and Baystate Health Services. He is a Fellow in the American College of Healthcare Executives and a Fellow and Life Member of the Healthcare Information and Management Systems Society. Mr. Rydell served as President of HIMSS and was a founding board member and Vice Chairman of the College of Healthcare Information Management Executives. Mr. Rydell is the co-author of the book, *The Physician-Computer Connection*.

Foreword

Conundrum indeed! Authors Bill Bria and Rich Rydell have been forced by conscience to write once again about the implementation of patient care information systems, this time in the form of a "conundrum" edition they hoped would be totally unnecessary. However, in the 12 years that have passed since publication of their first book, *The Physician-Computer Connection,* the connection has largely not been made and the conundrum has not been resolved. In fact, it has become much worse.

What is this conundrum? Simply stated, it is the disconnect between the highly computerized and networked world physicians live in and the grossly retarded state of computerization in most hospitals and health care settings where physicians work. Almost all physicians engage in technically complicated electronic transactions in their everyday life, like paying for gas at a pump or ordering goods over the Internet, but precious few enter medical orders into a computer. All but a few medical offices keep their patient records on paper, as do most hospitals. How can this be? In a world where cars and TVs are assembled on computer-controlled assembly lines, and where financial transactions are almost entirely electronic, how can life-or-death medical decisions still be dependent on the availability and legibility of voluminous paper records? We live in a world where the life or death of a patient can depend on whether an allergy sticker adheres to or falls off a chart. That is the conundrum in a nutshell.

The authors offer valuable insights into the underlying problem and detail the methods that have been successfully used to "get over it." They outline many pitfalls that lie in the way of a successful implementation and that contribute to the short professional tenures of many hospital CIOs, leading some to believe those initials actually stand for "Career Is Over." The importance to a successful implementation of clear organizational goals and committed leadership, rather than a particular technology, is repeated throughout the book. Deference to computer technocrats may work in pure science, but it usually leads to disaster in clinical medicine. After all, practicing physicians, nurses, and other professionals are the primary users of clinical information systems, not the technocrats. If a system does not fit into a medical professional's workflow, or if it slows them down significantly, it does not matter how technologically advanced the system is—the system will simply not be used. If it cost a lot of money, the prudent CIO will freshen up his resumé.

Bill Bria and Rich Rydell clearly articulate the key role that business logic plays in successful systems. They define business logic in healthcare as the characteristic "that captures and automates the workflow…communications and interactions between all members of the care delivery system." They note that business logic is the characteristic least likely to be apparent when commercial systems are evaluated, since it is much more complex than flashy on-screen graphics and nifty features more easily demonstrable to a receptive audience. But without valid medical business logic, a system will not match users' workflow needs and will fail, sometimes dangerously, in spite of the most advanced hardware and software features. That is just one part of the conundrum. Some of the most successful patient care information systems and computerized order entry systems in the United States still run in DOS, so that says something about the relative importance of technology versus enduring business logic.

The importance of training in successful implementations is stressed. Indeed, one example cited is a medical center that provided 61,000 hours of training to 13,000 caregivers, over a number of years.

The pace of implementation is also discussed, in terms of taking as much time as needed for an implementation to be successful rather than holding to an unrealistic schedule. The importance of involving key medical staff leaders in all parts of the system selection, development, and implementation process is described, even if that slows down the process. In spite of the problems there are many successful implementations and a number of them are used as examples in this book.

In terms of the future, the conundrum described may get worse before it gets better. Present day interns and residents have come through school using computers, PDAs, cell phones, and other electronic devices. As they begin service in most hospitals and clinics, they will not find computerized patient records or order entry systems— they will find paper, paper, and more paper. This will be the generation of doctors who will demand computerized records that are accessible all the time, in the hospital and out, over wires and wireless, always available. They will force us to make it happen, and they will contribute to the final product.

Finally, in terms of the future, one hopes that in a decade or so the authors can entertain and educate us once again, but with present day hobgoblins laid to rest. We look forward to the publication of *The Physician-Computer Collaboration,* which will celebrate the full integration of computers in physicians' professional lives.

M. Michael Shabot, M.D., FACS, FCCM FACMI
Medical Director
Surgical Intensive Care and Enterprise Information Services
Cedars-Sinai Medical Center
Professor of Surgery
David Geffen School of Medicine at UCLA
Los Angeles, California

Preface

In 1992 we wrote a book, *The Physician-Computer Connection*,[1] as a how-to guide for planning, selecting, implementing, and achieving effective physician use of patient care information systems (PCIS). Over the ensuing 14 years there has been a worldwide explosion of information technology such that now, 66 percent of American households whose respondent had attended graduate school reported owning a computer.[2]

The growth of the Internet has hastened the speed of information dissemination worldwide with an unprecedented egalitarianism that has been nothing less than astounding. Given our wired information age, the lack of similar growth in the daily use of information systems by clinicians in delivering healthcare in this country has been puzzling—and very disappointing. Consider: only 15 to 32 percent of hospitals have computerized provider order entry (CPOE) systems, and only 1.6 percent of hospitals required its use by providers.[3] This discrepancy has become even more frustrating in recent years when there has been a social and political focus on errors in medical care and a demonstration that information systems are a key answer to eliminating these errors.[4]

Although numerous articles have attempted to explain this puzzling discrepancy—or, as we call it, this conundrum—the purpose of this book is to help the healthcare information leader to motivate his/her organization to provide clinicians with a patient care information system. We will describe a phased, structured approach to implementing such systems successfully, employing proven strategies from both large and small healthcare systems from around the country. We base this approach, in part, on knowledge we have been privileged to gain over the last 20 years from networking with the best of this country's healthcare information technology leadership in such organizations as the Association of Medical Directors of Information Systems (www.amdis.org), the Healthcare Information and Management Systems Society (www.himss.org), the American Medical Informatics Association (www.amia.org), and many others.

We realize that in the current economic, political, and social climate, healthcare leaders face a daunting task in justifying the investments of time, resources, and costs required to implement a PCIS. Therefore, we will also endeavor in each step of this book to cite the best reference sources for information supporting a particular approach or strategy.

Furthermore, although our title reveals a bias of focus on physician use of clinical information systems, we realize that successful implementation of a PCIS today requires careful attention to the entire workflow and workforce of the modern healthcare system including nurses, allied health workers, administrators, and many others. Therefore, when addressing particular PCIS components that require careful balancing of workflow support for groups of knowledge workers (e.g., order communications), we will emphasize how and when each member of the patient care team needs to be supported from an information technology perspective.

Finally, although this book focuses on healthcare information technology, most of the recommendations and strategies will be independent of any particular technology. This is not simply our bias. As we believe can be easily demonstrated, the principles of achieving successful implementation of PCISs have remained remarkably constant over the past 30 years: excellent results have been achieved regardless of whether they were obtained in the era of the mainframe, minicomputer, personal computer, or now with the Internet. As will be discussed in Chapter 1, emphasis on technology itself is perhaps one of the most important reasons for delay in achieving the physician-computer connection in this country and one of the key reasons for the physician-computer conundrum—the failure in system implementation by and for healthcare providers.

Before we proceed, a word about words. In this book we use a number of acronyms for clinical systems. Please refer to Appendix B for a complete list of acronyms and their full meanings. All terminology is used to indicate the implementation of information systems in healthcare, including results reporting, order entry, documentation and many other functions.

With that said, welcome to *The Physician-Computer Conundrum*. Enjoy the ride, the chaos, and the illumination!

References

1. Bria W, Rydell R. *The Physician-Computer Connection: A Practical Guide to Physician Involvement in Hospital Information Systems.* Chicago, IL: AHA Books, 1992.
2. U.S. Bureau of the Census. *Statistical Abstract of the United States.* September, 1999.
3. Ash J, Gorman P, Lavelle M, et al. Investigating physician order entry in the field: lessons learned in a multi-center study. *Medinfo.* 2001, 10(pt 2):1107–1111.
4. Kohn LT, Corrigan JM, Donaldson MS, eds. *To Err is Human: Building a Safer Health System.* Institute of Medicine, Committee on Quality of Health Care in America. Washington, DC: National Academy Press, 2000.

CHAPTER 1

A Road Map to a Successful Patient Care Information System

For a patient care information system (PCIS) to be implemented successfully, it is important to understand how such a system is structured and appreciate its complexity. After our own successful (and not so successful) experiences over the last 25 years in this area, the following structure appears to make the most sense. It includes the most important factors in the development and successful implementation of PCISs. Our discussions with other clinical and IT leaders from around the country and the world confirm that the tenets of each of these elements—what we term a road map to a successful PCIS—seem to hold true.

In this chapter we describe three different pathways within this overall road map. We define the pathways and outline the stages of each. We emphasize repeatedly the individual importance of each of these pathways as well as their key interdependence. That interdependence will become clearer as we proceed, but it also illustrates the significant challenge of overcoming the physician-computer conundrum. The complexity and interdependence of these pathways is a prime reason why overcoming the physician-computer conundrum presents such a significant challenge.

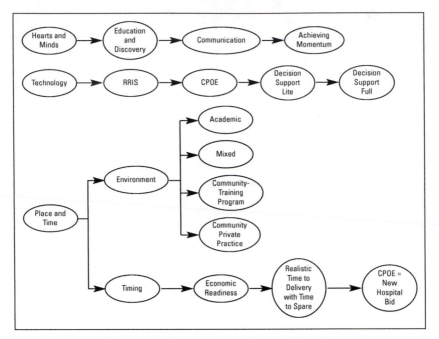

Figure 1-1. Roadmap to a Successful PCIS.

The three main pathways on this roadmap to a successful PCIS are: (1) what we call "winning hearts and minds;" (2) technology; and (3) environment and timing (Figure 1-1).

HEARTS AND MINDS

The hearts and minds pathway identifies the essential learning, both by individuals (leadership in particular) as well as organizations, that must occur for a PCIS to be implemented successfully. Within this path, there are three important stages: (1) education and discovery; (2) communication; and (3) achieving momentum.

Education and Discovery

The education and discovery phase must include individuals within an organization who are to be formally involved and charged with leading a PCIS project. There is no substitute for the education of project leaders, even those who may have had previous experience in clinical information systems, when considering a PCIS for an entire organization. Firsthand knowledge by these individuals will serve them and their organization extremely well over time as they can gain confidence in their directly-observed experience as well as "get the real story" at successful sites from around the country.

Consider this first phase of winning hearts and minds—education and discovery—as a *breeding ground* for champions for your PCIS project within your organization. During this phase, readings in both peer-reviewed and other literature on PCISs projects are usually distributed. Direct person-to-person contact must also be arranged and achieved. This person-to-person contact is best performed by peers, that is, physician-to-physician, nurse-to-nurse, administrator-to-administrator, to overcome some of the initial concerns and barriers to effective communication that can appear when addressing the complexity of approaching a PCIS from a technological standpoint.

We mention education and discovery in this category because it is essential that the "important people" and PCIS champions within your organization have an epiphany. These individuals must discover for themselves the value of proceeding on this difficult but important path of implementing a PCIS. This discovery may simply be, in fact, a validation of benefits that had previously been published widely. It may, however, also be a particular nuance of a PCIS project's benefits and organizational values that will allow a particular individual to become an enthusiastic and effective champion for your organization.

Site visits are often mentioned in this pathway and can be quite helpful. However, it is important that trips and site visits be arranged and set up properly. Specifically, expectations for achieving goals of education and discovery should be clearly outlined and researched before site visits are made. This is important because of one fundamental fact: Any site with an existing PCIS has certain elements that shine and of which the organization is proud. Likewise, every site with an implemented PCIS also has elements that the organization would just as soon not emphasize. If there is a mismatch between the site's best characteristics and visitors' expectations, then instead of motivating champions, the site visit will result in dissatisfaction, a sense of wasted time, and a diminution of enthusiasm for the project.

Education and discovery can certainly include communications with vendor representatives as well as customers of the systems. However, the ancient warning of *buyer beware* is never more relevant than in the complex and standard poor environment of commercial PCIS. Education and discovery, therefore, are important beginnings on the journey of implementing a PCIS.

Certainly as a PCIS project proceeds, there are different layers of information that need to be revealed. Other information is reevaluated as it becomes altered by experience. For example, interest in the features of a PCIS that include clinical decision support are initially items of keen interest during many early experiences with PCIS. However, as individuals gain knowledge and experience, it becomes clear that decision support tools are a double-edged sword that may not only enhance medical decision making, but if poorly designed, may interfere with it. It is therefore essential that the PCIS project director carefully pace the learning for the group as well as allow relationships that foster information exchange to be established that will last throughout the years of the project.

Communication

The second phase of the hearts and minds pathway is communication. Communication of the information gained through site visits, literature, and personal communications is an essential process even in the smallest of organizations. From the standpoint of providing a concise but clear body of knowledge for all who will be affected by the introduction of a PCIS, it is essential to employ effective and, again, paced strategies of communication. For example, at the outset of a PCIS project, conferences, symposia, grand rounds, and other large forum settings are often helpful in sharing information with large groups in an organization. However, other communications media, such as newsletters (both print and e-mail) and focus groups, can also be used effectively to disseminate the detailed information necessary to bring staff and faculty along as a PCIS project proceeds.

As was mentioned above in discussing the education and discovery phase, communication is an opportunity to allow individuals to "get it." That is, individuals provided with the same information will identify different specific elements in that information that are meaningful and relevant to them. These particular elements will help them to understand as well as accept the changes necessary to effectively assimilate and utilize a PCIS. For example, nurses may identify within a PCIS project the value of nursing-specific clinical documentation in a system as well as the value to nursing of having legible ordering through computerized provider order entry (CPOE). Physicians, however, may see the importance and value of having an electronic medical record (EMR) for remote management of patients in hospitals, from offices, or even from home. Finally, administration may understand the value of a PCIS from the business perspective of automatic charge capture on ordering that a PCIS system can provide.

These personalized communications and epiphanies take time to evolve. Continuing to provide information about the PCIS project is essential throughout the course of a project. However, there is one caveat: Building enthusiasm and expectations for a PCIS too soon can result in disbelief on the part of staff and faculty that a project will ever be completed. Therefore, there is a fine balance in communication between the amount of information, pacing of the release of that information, and providing sufficient information so that individuals can personalize and understand the value of a PCIS from their individual perspectives.

Achieving Momentum

Achieving—and maintaining—momentum is an ultimate goal in the process of winning hearts and minds in a PCIS project. Momentum can be understood within an organization as essentially achieving agreement on direction so that a project can be carried forward and survive over time and budget periods and against competing projects. Momentum has been achieved when there is sufficient agreement among an organization's leadership and rank and file that a PCIS project is indeed worthwhile and is important for the organization to achieve its business and clinical goals.

Building this momentum at a proper level and pace within an organization is more art than science. Level of momentum speaks to the importance of enthusiasm for a PCIS project by an organization's top leadership and executive cabinet for the project to continue to have sufficient financial support and business focus to succeed. Pacing of momentum for a PCIS project speaks to the realization that if expectations of a delivery are set too soon—or if espoused delivery dates for system implementation are too far in the future—then faculty and staff may either develop disappointment or indifference, respectively, to a project's implementation.

Such pacing is especially important in PCISs because there are natural benchmarks of interest that must be recognized within a project. These milestones, for example, include selection of the initial system, organization of focus groups for system configuration and design, dissemination of system training to faculty and staff, and, of course, final implementation. Depending upon an organization's size, these stages may be separated by weeks or many months. Hence, the need for proper pacing of enthusiasm and momentum for a PCIS project to sustain an appropriate level of involvement and expectation throughout the project through delivery.

TECHNOLOGY

The second pathway on the roadmap to a successful PCIS is PCIS technology. There are logical technology milestones in the progress towards a PCIS that are important for the clinical champion, project leader, and chief information officer (CIO) to recognize. The technological stages of a PCIS may be divided into four steps, each of which is discussed below:

1. A results reporting information system (RRIS);
2. A computerized clinician order entry system;
3. Decision support systems (DSS), initially with two subtypes: decision support system lite and robust; and
4. A knowledge-based information environment.

Results Reporting Information Systems: Characteristics

A results reporting information system (RRIS) is both the most common type of PCIS available in American hospitals today and, not coincidentally, the easiest to implement.

The automation of healthcare can be understood as processes that involve information gathering, analysis, communication, refinement, and completion. Although the current national debate on reduction of errors in medicine[1] focuses on CPOE, there is only one element of this information process that physicians and patients appreciate as beneficial. Indeed, the delivery of complete, organized, timely, and usable medical information by a well-crafted RRIS is both easier to implement and more rapidly adopted by healthcare workers than other systems.

In this section, we describe the key elements of an RRIS and the most important factors contributing to the achievement of maximum benefits. After describing an RRIS's characteristics, we then illustrate them with an example of an RRIS, the *Care Web* system, that has been implemented at the University of Michigan Medical Center. Because this section focuses on the key information strategies necessary to achieve success in creating and implementing an RRIS, key technologies such as clinical data repositories (CDRs) and interface/integration strategies (interface engines, for example) are mentioned only to aid in illustrating the clinician and user-based discussion.

The five key functional characteristics of an RRIS are

1. Accuracy;
2. Timeliness;
3. Patient centricity;
4. Comprehensiveness; and
5. Presentation flexibility.

Let us examine each of these.

RRIS Characteristics: Accuracy

In the complex world of modern American healthcare, although information accuracy is imperative, it is not a given feature of an information system. Rather, it is one that must continually be tested and pursued. There are a number of reasons for this, including the lack of information integration in American healthcare; the mobility of modern society; and the complexity of testing technology, with rapid growth of new tests and new methods of performing old studies.

One of the greatest frustrations Americans have with healthcare is the poor integration of services. This includes everything from poor interphysician communication, lack of coordination of primary through secondary and tertiary care, and finally, the frustrating confusion among the clinical, administrative, and financial aspects of healthcare delivery. These elements have arisen in the current mosaic of managed care, fee-for-service, community, and integrated delivery systems that comprise the healthcare environment in the United States today. The reader has only to recall anyone in his/her family who has required care at multiple clinical settings or, worse, different healthcare institutions, to realize that healthcare testing and information standards are not yet a prominent feature of the delivery system. Because of this reality, RRIS systems are challenged to ensure that such mundane issues as normal lab test ranges, test result terminologies, and so forth are properly normalized. This becomes particularly important as one considers the mobility of American society and the need to understand medical information trends across time, systems, and locales.

With respect to mobility, not only are we faced with massively decentralized healthcare needs (for example, continuing chemotherapy protocols begun in Boston while the patient travels to a winter home in Arizona), but also with diseases that actually have been facilitated by travel technology (for example, tuberculosis or deep venous thrombosis). Information accuracy and delivery is becoming progressively more important, as historical information must travel with the patient. This is especially imperative for people requiring care of acute problems (allergies, for instance), and for those requiring continuing care of chronic diseases (AIDS, malignancy). It is also essential to realize that the propagation of information technology in many other industries, and society's expectation of its availability, only serve to heighten the issue of the need for providing essential clinical information accurately and across locales.

Finally, the ever-changing technology of medical testing itself presents an important challenge to the provision of accurate information in an RRIS. For example, as of this writing, there are no less than four separate and distinct technologies employed at major medical centers for the measurement of blood sugars. Although results are similar using the modalities, normal ranges are not identical, making accurate reporting and trending a challenge. Understanding all sources of information in an RRIS, as a means of achieving true accuracy of information recording and reporting, is more challenging and important than ever.

RRIS Characteristics: Timeliness

Due to the continuous cost pressures of routine ambulatory care in the United States, leisurely doctor-patient meetings of the past have now become intensively time-pressured, with 10- to 15-minute interactions common. With this amazing compression of communication time, if the patient and physician are not working with the same up-to-date information, then at best delays in care will occur; at worst, errors will be made. Frustration with obtaining access to care remains one of the most important concerns of patients and physicians alike.[1] Access is also a key element in the perception of improved quality and safety of care. An RRIS must deliver the latest information at the point of care in order to meet expectations of timely medical decision making and quality care.

RRIS Characteristics: Patient Centricity

Patient centricity refers to large-scale data and information integration across the continuum of care. In 2003 the *New York Times* quoted the chief academic officer at Harvard Medical School's Partners Health Care as saying that the reduction in cardiac death rates was "one of the great triumphs of medicine in the past 50 years."[2] The article also stated that so few Americans are dying of myocardial infarction (MI) and stroke that rates can no longer be calculated. Patients are now surviving into their 60s, 70s, and beyond, only to have chronic heart disease with congestive heart failure.

This trend—converting previously life-ending diseases to chronic diseases—has occurred across a broad spectrum of conditions from heart disease to cancer. Therefore, the reality of modern ambulatory care practice is the care of patients over many years, some with complex diseases with exacerbations and remissions that require the monitoring of trends. The conversion of our information sources from episode-based to continuous and patient-centered has occurred slowly.

RRIS Characteristics: Comprehensiveness

In addition to the challenges of information integration from disparate healthcare systems and geographic locations, the challenge of patient care has been compounded by chronic diseases that are much more common, and that require clinicians to have the perspective of years (sometimes decades) of information from the RRIS in order to identify and treat them. Therefore, besides lab trends and archives of reports, the modern RRIS must have an accurate and continually updated diagnosis and patient problem list to allow clinicians to recognize everything from recurrence of old problems to drug disease interactions before they become real problems.

RRIS Characteristics: Presentation Flexibility

The fifth key functional characteristic of an RRIS is presentation flexibility, i.e., facilitation of the conversion of data into information. The RRIS must present large amounts of information on individual patients over time. This will allow the physician to have a better understanding of trends and patterns to discover the source of patient problems, as well as patient responses to treatments.

To achieve the myriad of applications, tests, and evaluations, the RRIS must provide an unprecedented degree of flexibility. The user must be able to easily construct recognized patterns of disease so that if a diagnostic profile exists, it will become apparent in the RRIS display. For example, a patient with chest pain usually requires blood work in the emergency department. The pattern of the so-called enzymes allows the physician to identify those individuals who are having dangerous, immediate heart muscle injury, as well as those who have chest pain due to other less catastrophic causes. The RRIS should allow the easy online display of the panel of tests allowing immediate recognition of problems by the clinician.

The modern RRIS must allow for display of test data in a manner that alerts to more than simple high or low results. One requirement for the system (or its source systems) is that it must have the ability to identify and display delta values or greater-than-expected changes in test results even though the absolute values may still be within the normal range. For example, a patient may experience a fall in blood count immediately after a biopsy procedure that results in an absolute figure that is at the lower limit of normal, constituting an important warning that a possible continuing bleeding mishap has occurred.

RRIS Example: Care Web

Care Web illustrates the transformation of an integrated healthcare delivery system by an RRIS. In 1997, the University of Michigan

Hospitals and Health Systems (UMHHS), with which we are affiliated, took stock of its clinical information environment both to assess impending Y2K issues and to formulate a new strategy for the coming millennium. We found that the clinical information catalog consisted of more than 400 applications supported in over 60 departments in the medical center. It was clear that this situation resulted in increased support costs and maintenance for the organization. Even more troubling was the fact that these systems duplicated basic functions such as information retrieval and presentation. This analysis made it evident that a patient-centric RRIS built upon a central data repository was needed.

At that time, fortuitously, programming expertise in Web-based architecture was growing at the medical center information technology department (MCIT) under the direction of Dr. Jocelyn DeWitt, CIO at UMHHS. The Web technology was attractive because it was evident that the architecture could provide rapid accessibility, require little training, and, it was hoped, decrease the cost of maintenance by standardizing systems, both from the standpoint of information access and integration, thereby avoiding the mass duplication of information access in the existing environment.

The new system was dubbed *Care Web*. Development proceeded with the goals of increased patient throughput, standardization, and safety. The system was developed in incremental steps directed at specific information problems or issues within the organization. For example, the first problem was how to combine information from a legacy homegrown patient scheduling system with the data from a new commercial scheduling system. The vendor had no product to integrate our legacy system, so *Care Web* was given the task, which it performed admirably.

The key advantage of the *Care Web* system was the development of the central data repository with what might be called opportunistic information integration, or acquisition of information from legacy systems in whatever manner was possible. For the more robust system, standards-based (Health Level Seven [HL7], for example) communications were utilized. Where much smaller systems were encountered, file transfer protocol (FTP) batch data transfers were used. Most importantly, the user interface was designed to be as Web-standard and familiar to any browser user as possible.

The system was first released in 1998, and within the following eight months it became the clinical information resource for both the inpatient and outpatient enterprise (Figure 1-2). A survey of house staff, attending physicians, nurses, allied healthcare workers, and the administrative users (over 10,000 total) was performed in 1998 to evaluate why users were adopting this system so rapidly and completely. The top reasons for user satisfaction were

- All clinical information in one place;
- Ease of use;
- Familiarity of the Web user interface; and
- Incremental growth of the system.

Incremental growth was possible due to a remarkable synergy that developed with the medical, nursing, and administrative staff as *Care Web* grew in popularity. A *Care Web* steering committee (consisting of chair-appointed representatives from each constituency) remains the main organizational body reviewing, prioritizing, and assisting in the management of *Care Web* development. The multidisciplinary committee increased the interest, excitement, and ownership of the system by the institution at large.

Since 1998, *Care Web* has continued to grow into areas beyond traditional results reporting (documentation, for example), and it now exists as the primary means for clinical information editing and electronic signature. Physicians and others access it via the Web from offices, homes, and the field using secure socket and double-blind password technology.

Attribution is always a difficult issue with information systems. However, over the past six years of *Care Web's* existence the following benefits have been observed:

- A reduction in average length of stay (ALOS) (Figure 1-3);
- Compliance with rapid document signature by clinicians; and
- A marked increase in pediatric immunization rates (Figure 1-4).

For these reasons, the University of Michigan named *Care Web* Program of the Year in 2001.

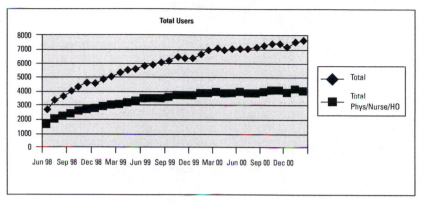

Figure 1-2. Growth of *Care Web* Use: 1998–2000.

RRIS: Conclusion

RRIS is the key first step toward clinical decision support in any healthcare enterprise. Its advantages of improved patient care and IT resource consolidation are now facilitated by the existence and popularity of the Internet. With data integration and communication standards, the process of creating a CDR is an essential first infrastructure step. It is also important to gain the trust, attention, and interest of your organization and medical staff in particular. An enterprisewide RRIS strategy is, we believe, an excellent step on the way toward the electronic medical record (EMR).

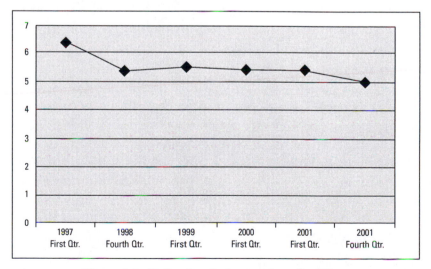

Figure 1-3. Reduction in Average Length of Stay.

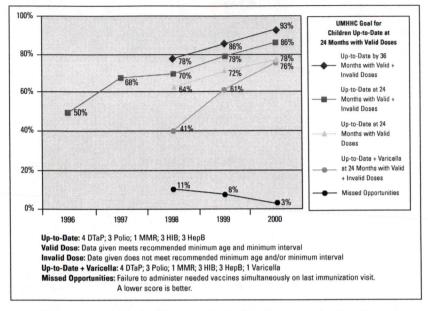

Figure 1-4. A Marked Increase in Pediatric Immunization Rates.

The RRIS, because of its features of information integration, clear method to clinical practice, improved time and efficiency, and performance for an entire healthcare organization, provides a wonderful first introduction to PCIS for an organization. However, it is important for reasons that will become obvious that this is an introduction rather than the end of this story.

Computerized Provider Order Entry

The next logical step in the technological pathway towards a successful PCIS is clinician computerized order entry. Although these systems go by many names, the most common in the literature today is a computerized provider order entry or CPOE system. Obviously, the focus of these systems is the capture, communication, and completion of the order process that is most often first described and implemented as an inpatient system. However, more and more healthcare is being provided in an ambulatory care setting with shortened lengths of hospital stays. Therefore, CPOE continues to take on added importance throughout the continuum of inpatient and outpatient care.

Many excellent reviews have been published on CPOE systems and, thanks to organizations such as AMIA, HIMSS, and AMDIS, there is a growing body of knowledge about systems structured with necessary functions and, even more recently, standards of comparison. We will not discuss these elements further at this time except to note that CPOE remains the most elusive second step in the successful implementation of a PCIS in American healthcare today. Reasons for this will be discussed in Chapter 2. Suffice it to say, all of the necessary preparatory steps listed in pathway one of winning hearts and minds and pathway three of environment and timing need to be brought to bear to successfully follow through with this second technological step in implementing PCIS of CPOE.

Decision Support Systems

A decision support system (DSS) is one that brings to bear one or two elements of patient-specific information to aid in decision making for the ordering clinician. For example, a system that automatically includes kidney function and presence of the diagnosis of diabetes mellitus to an ordering clinician at the time of consideration of a radiographic study including iodine-based dye that could cause renal insufficiency can—and has—been shown to avoid significant patient mishap.

Avoiding the hyperbole of clinical information system marketing, DSSs are not simply alerts. Alerts are most often implemented in commercial systems as "one size fits all" triggers in hopes of presenting useful information at a decision point. For example, an alert would let a clinician know that a patient had a critically low laboratory value such as a blood count or hematocrit, suggesting that a risk of bleeding or other cause of anemia was present. However, this alert information, particularly in an inpatient setting, is usually redundant to the normal review process that clinicians perform. Furthermore, excessive alerts that neither adapt to a clinician's particular practice style, nor take into account or patient-specific elements such as diagnosis and other co-morbidities, may only achieve annoyance for the user or even worse, be ignored on a routine basis. Therefore, DSSs are far more sophisticated than simple alerts and can provide necessary patient-specific data just in time.

In this pathway, DSSs initially may include simple strategies, such as a DSS lite, or more robust strategies to achieve this goal. For example, a decision support lite system would perform the functions listed previously as an example of DSS. A DSS robust system could, in addition, recognize risks for populations within a region or with particular diagnoses and present this information to the ordering physician at the appropriate time. And a DSS that automatically tracks the most likely organisms responsible for empiric critical care diagnoses such as sepsis, community-acquired pneumonia, wound infections, and others, could cross-correlate this information with the most likely organisms for infection with the most likely antibiotics successful in treating those organisms as measured by a particular clinical laboratory in that region for a previous time period.

In this manner, a more robust clinical DSS would have the potential for improving empiric antibiotic selection not only from a cost-effective and formulary control perspective, but, most importantly, from a clinical benefit perspective. In fact, such a system has been extensively reported from Latter-Day Saints Hospital (LDS) in Salt Lake City, Utah.[3] Although this pathway is being discussed from the perspective of specific elements of technology, there are extremely important components of successful development and implementation of DSSs that include considerations of local clinical consensus, input into the creation and deployment of these systems, as well as alignment with an agenda for change outlined by clinical leadership.

An excellent recent summary[4] of clinical DSSs emphasized that there is a cycle of clinical information and learning within an organization that is the ultimate technological step in a PCIS pathway. Thus, DSSs are an incremental step towards achieving a true knowledge-based information environment.

Knowledge-Based Systems

A knowledge-based information environment can be described as one that includes a cycle of information and learning. This cycle begins with capturing the actual process of care in order writing and communication. Step two of the cycle involves quality improvement review of the outcomes of care, for example, for a diagnosis such as pneumonia, an evaluation of the success rate of therapy of a community-acquired pneumonia using a particular combination of medications. Third, a knowledge-based environment would incorporate information from clinical research, consensus reports, and expert panel reviews of recommended approaches to diagnoses such as community-acquired pneumonia into a rules engine.

A rules engine, far more sophisticated than an alert engine alone, would incorporate specific important bits of information specific to a patient that would be incorporated into a recommendation at the point of care. For example, a rules engine could bring to bear several separate bits of patient data, such as alcoholism plus community-acquired pneumonia increases risk for atypical organisms and higher mortality with a pneumonia.

As the fourth and final phase of a knowledge-based information system, the collection of rules is then incorporated into the actual order entry system so that every patient meeting the criteria relevant to a rule set has the benefit of the knowledge gained by examining previous outcomes or previous cases. In this way, for example, rather than simply publishing guidelines for a chronic condition such as asthma, there would be a specific recommendation at the outset of hospitalization for acute asthma, recognizing whether or not a patient had been on appropriate care prior to hospitalization and emphasizing the institution of that care at the time of discharge. Needless to say, while examples of successfully implemented CPOE systems in America are uncommon, fully implemented knowledge-based systems are unknown. This simply attests to the time necessary to achieve this goal as well as the commitment and technological sophistication of an information environment necessary to achieve it. Nevertheless, there are growing examples of evolving knowledge-based information systems throughout the country,[4] and therefore the reader should be heartened that the pursuit of a knowledge-based environment is an ongoing challenge and one that still requires the innovation, commitment, and enthusiasm to reach fulfillment.

PLACE AND TIME

The final pathway on the road map to a successful PCIS involves the twin elements of environment and timing. These components are not so much modifiable at the whim or will of project directors, clinical champions, or others involved in the PCIS project; rather, they are important elements to be recognized by those groups to achieve success in implementation. Let us first examine environment.

Environment

Since the beginning of PCIS implementation literature, it has been recognized that the environment in which these systems are implemented can help determine the outcome. For example, recognition that larger centers would have more challenges than would small community hospitals toward mobilizing faculty, staff, and necessary support for such systems has been postulated and proven true repeatedly.

However, as medicine and healthcare delivery systems have become more sophisticated and complex, so has the impact of environment as an element in the road map toward successful PCIS implementation. For example, in a recent widely published PCIS implementation failure, the impact of busy community physicians on the retraction of a CPOE system has been reported.[5] In this case specific problems arose when physicians in a busy Los Angeles community practice found persistent difficulty in both the efficiency and complexity of an extremely well-designed CPOE system. Additionally, in light of the fact that more and more medical care is being driven through the ambulatory care arena, there is increased emphasis on linking clinics and offices into PCIS systems as a success factor in implementation of a PCIS.

It is clear, however, that overall, the American healthcare scene—with its entire economic environment, shorter average office visit time, and increased administration and bureaucratic overhead of practice of medicine—has led to less and less tolerance for the needed learning and accommodation of the change of implementing a PCIS regardless of setting: ambulatory, inpatient, or otherwise. So it is with the debate regarding errors in medicine: Physicians and patient groups alike recognize that automation plays a role in the solution to the perceived problems of increased medical errors today as published by the Institute of Medicine (IOM); however, in a recent survey neither physicians nor patients prioritized automation in the top 10 solutions for this nationally perceived problem.[6]

Therefore, old assumptions about environment, such as that house officers are vastly easier to incorporate into PCIS training than community physicians, or that smaller centers will consistently be easier to deal with than large centers, still hold true in general. However, in specific cases due to the changes in practice of medicine in recent years, there are additional challenges across the board in understanding, modifying, and absorbing the changes in medical practice necessary to successfully use automation or PCIS.

Timing

The second component of the pathway in the road map to a successful PCIS is timing. Organizational timing speaks to several issues that can make or break the success of a PCIS. These include (1) economic readiness; (2) realistic time frame to deliver, with necessary slack or spare time included; and (3) stability of organizational leadership and focus on the PCIS as a key strategic program.

Economic readiness is, as mentioned above, a challenge for all healthcare organizations endeavoring to embark on the purchase, design, and implementation of a PCIS in this country today. The tighter margins of medical care, the rising costs of commercial PCIS systems, and the need (particularly in larger organizations) for PCIS projects to span many years, compound the challenges. To recognize that the modern Internet era has both aided the PCIS project manager as well as complicated his/her work is a fair statement. That is, the Web has contributed to people's perception of a free and open medium with low overhead providing significant benefits in information retrieval, dissemination, and collection. However, the specific but limited vertical market of healthcare information systems is only just beginning to realize some of the benefits of the information architecture standardization that have come about in the era of the World Wide Web. The vertical market of healthcare information systems is therefore just beginning to realize cost efficiencies of standardization as witnessed by the experience of the Veterans Administration's computer-based patient record system (CPRS) that has been implemented nationwide. An additional important component of the timing pathway in the successful implementation of a PCIS is setting a realistic time frame for system delivery with adequate time to spare. This fact has been illustrated by the published experience of the Ohio State University (OSU) where this large healthcare information integrated system's implementation of a PCIS was delayed for years by Y2K-related considerations.[7] Nonetheless, with the perseverance of leadership in that organization, the system was eventually completed successfully.

The final component in the timing pathway is the consideration of stability of healthcare organization leadership and the need for its steadfast commitment to implementation of a PCIS. Timing here is a balancing act. It is well understood that the average tenure of chief information officers in American healthcare systems today is less than two years. This does not match well with the reality of durations of larger organizations' PCIS implementations that can stretch from five to nine years or more. Hence it can be seen that timing may be particularly challenging when the leadership that was responsible for the initial design of a PCIS project, the agreement on the project's cost, and the commitment to seeing a project through are likely not to be the same team that will be in office by the time a PCIS system is in fact completed.

Certainly this concern in the pathway toward successful PCIS implementation can be completely obviated by a steadfast, consistent, and committed leadership team that does not change significantly over the duration, but again, this is all too infrequently the case. There are, however, strategies to mitigate this risk of timing, not the least of which is the orientation, education, and communication to faculty and staff of an organization in order to regularly revalidate the priority and importance of a PCIS project to new leadership over the years.

After examining these three major interdependent pathways toward a successful PCIS implementation—hearts and minds, technology, and environment and timing—we have the fundamentals of the structure necessary for success in the American healthcare scene today. While these elements provide reliable and time-testing tenets of success, there are numerous pitfalls that can beset the PCIS project director and team. It is the identification of these prototypical pitfalls and their remediation or avoidance that are the topics of our next chapter.

References

1. Kohn LT, Corrigan JM, Donaldson MS, eds. *To Err Is Human: Building a Safer Health System.* Institute of Medicine, Committee on Quality of Health Care in America. Washington, DC: National Academy Press, 2000.

2. Kolata G. Gains on heart disease leave more survivors, and questions. *New York Times.* January 19, 2003.

3. Postotniks SL, Classen DC, Evans RS, et al. Implementing antibiotic practice guidelines through computer-assisted decision support: clinical and financial outcomes. *Ann Intern Med.* 1996, 124(10)884–890.

4. Bates D, Cohen M, Leape L, et al. Reducing the frequency of errors in medicine using information technology. *J Am Med Inform Assoc.* 2001, 8:299–308.

5. Chin T. Doctors pull plug on paperless system. *American Medical News.* February 17, 2003.

6. Blendon RJ, DesRoches CM, Brodie M, et al. Views of practicing physicians and the public on medical errors. *N Engl J Med.* 2002, 347(24):1933–1940.

7. Murff HJ, Kannry J. Physician satisfaction with two order entry systems. *J Am Med Inform Assoc.* 2001, 8:499–511.

Chapter 2

Pitfalls and How to Avoid Them

When you consider the number of ways a computerized provider order entry (CPOE) project can go horribly wrong, there are a number of stereotypical scenarios that the reader is strongly advised to recognize and avoid at all costs. We present the following catalog as cautionary tales from personal as well as vicarious sad experience, a "rogues' gallery," if you will, of CPOE pitfalls. They include

- Revenge of the nerds
- So easy a CEO can do it!
- One size fits all!
- Install CPOE while you sleep!
- This technology is the answer, man!
- CPOE as Sherman's march to the sea
- Controlling your medical staff is easy!

REVENGE OF THE NERDS

Since most people, when first considering a CPOE project, will assume that knowledge of technology is of paramount importance, one of the most common of all CPOE pitfalls is to delegate project control and decision making to the techno elite, so-called "geeks" or "nerds." Although there can be little question that technology must play a role in the CPOE acquisition and implementation process, one of the most reliable means for a project to fail is to subordinate leadership knowledgeable about the actual operations, key personnel, and politics of an organization to a group of technocrats. Although the domain of CPOE is obviously based in an information technology, the matching of a system, developed or purchased, has much more to do with the fundamental knowledge of the organization and staff that are anticipated to be changed by the introduction of such a system, rather than the fundamentals of a particular CPOE technology itself.

Proof that myriad technologies can produce a very successful CPOE system is evident worldwide. Mainframe, client server, PC-based, and now Web-based systems have all been implemented, with no single approach being proven clearly more successful than any other. Indeed, medicine itself has yielded many recurrent lessons of where, for example, older treatments (such as diuretics for hypertension) have proven over time to be superior to new medications. So it is with CPOE technologies: Provided a modicum of stability and functionality, systems can prove successful regardless of platform.

Warning Signs

Why is it, then, that otherwise astute and perspicacious healthcare leaders will relinquish control and direction to technologists in CPOE projects? The answer probably lies in the intimidating impact technology has had on society. Evidence of the social effects of the relentless pace of technological change is reflected in numerous articles on the "digital divide" that now exists.[1] This divide has been used by many as a tool of both intimidation and power. Unfortunately, we are now realizing that technology is not the unalloyed boon that many had hoped it would be.

One of the key indicators that this stereotypical pitfall is in motion is when a CPOE project's key requirements are defined in "techno-speak" terms rather than plain English. When the top 10 requirements for an organization's CPOE system include "Open architecture technology employing java and CCOW," you know you've gone off the deep end. Balancing the need to define and prioritize the key functions of a system against the underlying technologies necessary to achieve those goals is a collaborative effort between CPOE leadership and technologist.

Cures

What needs to be established early in this dialogue is the primacy of the *organizational goals and priorities of the project,* rather than the importance of a particular enabling technology. The technological approach must make sense within the context of structural and functional requirements of the organization and people expected to use the CPOE. Understanding and achieving this balance has been the deciding factor in innumerable CPOE projects over the past 30 years.

SO EASY A CEO CAN DO IT!

In the rogues' gallery of pitfalls, this one is the most insidious. Insidious, because at first blush, it makes all the sense in the world to include organizational leaders, e.g., the chief of staff, CEO, and senior management, as top level chairs of CPOE selection and implementation committees. Certainly, without the support and involvement of individuals in these positions, a CPOE project will not have the political, sustained organizational, and even financial support it needs to be successful. It is in fact important that a proper *CPOE board* be identified so that the project has the needed support in the aforementioned areas.

Warning Signs

However, if an unhappy series of coincidences occurs, the advantage of having top leadership on your CPOE Board of Directors can turn into a complete nightmare guaranteed to at least complicate your project, if not destroy it altogether. The elements of this unhappiness are (1) presence of a strong organizational leader in a decision-making role in the CPOE project; (2) this same individual or individuals having absolutely no experience in healthcare information technology; and (3) the combination of excitement and firm conviction by this individual(s) that by (a) reading the literature, (b) attending several national meetings on the subject, and/or (c) networking with national colleagues they can muster all of the necessary skills and knowledge in short order to slam a CPOE in place! Yes, if you find yourself at risk of this pitfall, without some very quick and deft political maneuvering, you will find yourself with a dead CPOE project. However, it may take months or even years for the death to be final. During that time you will have the agony of reliving every bad decision that has ever been made in the history of healthcare IT systems, including these classics: (1) "Let's just go to a famous CPOE site and repeat their success with same software!"; (2) "You know, I've just read this great article and it says what we really should do is . . .;" and the very popular (3) "You say that a CPOE system must cost $X, but I've just talked to my friend in Boston and he has the best system in the country and only spent $1/10!"

Cures

As is true in most of human medicine, prevention and avoidance are far easier and definitely preferable to treatment where this pitfall is concerned. For example, it is certainly important to include your organizational leadership in the CPOE effort, but for heaven's sake, *manage them*! Whether you are the CIO or physician lead, *partner* with this person or persons and ensure that your take on matters is always clear to them. When a major newsbyte is shared in the boardroom, it can make all the difference that you are the next person aware of it and can keep the CPOE ship sailing along smoothly.

There are a number of ways to establish this important credibility and relationship with your leader or leadership group at risk: (1) tailored site visit; (2) have him/her attend your national meeting on CPOE/IT; and (3) provide opportunities for creativity within a project that would not put the entire CPOE effort at jeopardy, e.g., pilot projects.

Tailored site visits warrant some additional explanation. All too often, CPOE project groups are shipped off to vendor demonstration sites that are either inappropriate or in worst cases blatantly disastrous. There are several reasons for this problem including the reality that vendors often try to promote demonstration sites that have a pleased senior leader who continues to buy their products, rather than performing an analysis of what your CPOE project team really *needs and wants* to see.

One way to avoid this is to what we call "surgically select" a series of sites and *prepare* your CPOE team leaders, setting appropriate expectations on what the visits will yield as well as emphasizing what should be learned from each site. For example, a nontechnical senior physician, a chief of staff, should visit a mature CPOE implementation site that has been using a CPOE system to implement important quality of care initiatives for years, as a means of understanding why the technology would be worthwhile for your organization.

Conversely, the technologists on your CPOE project team should attend the vendor's development center and see not only the current vendor development team but be allowed in on the vendor's future development plans. In this manner, you can allow the individuals on your CPOE team to learn about the systems in their own time frame, in a way they will understand and, importantly, in a manner that you can manage and ensure that your project moves in a positive direction for the benefit of your entire organization.

ONE SIZE FITS ALL!

In the world of healthcare IT, there are many myths born of our frustration with the reality of the gap between available technologies and what we hoped would already be available. Some of these myths are reflected in often-heard statements like these:

1. "Surely someone must have already developed the computer system that does this;"
2. "My goodness, with the ease of use of current computer systems, we shouldn't have to spend time and money on configuring or designing a new system ourselves;"
3. "By now your company must have accumulated all the benefits of your hundreds of installations making our effort so much easier!"
4. "We understand you have a computer system that never goes down;" or
5. "You said you've had 25 years experience with configuring and installing these systems, but the implementation team you sent are younger than my kids!"

Warning Signs

One maladaptive reaction to the aforementioned (and many other) disappointments with the existing healthcare IT vendor industry is the pursuit of success with what we call the "General Purpose IT

Company." This pitfall may take different forms, including these: (1) "My cousin runs this banking IT company and...;" or (2) "I've been totally unimpressed with the current healthcare IT vendors so I've contacted SUPERBIG SYSTEMS and they're interested in working with us to develop a new generation system!"

Cures

Both versions of this pitfall ignore one core truth: "It's the business logic, stupid." Business logic is probably the single most important asset of a healthcare IT system. It is also probably the most poorly understood component of systems by the naïve customer. We have developed the following definition:

> Business logic is that characteristic of a healthcare IT system that captures and automates the workflow and complexity of communications and interactions between all members of the care delivery system.

The more you consider that statement, the greater the magnitude of understanding. Certainly in the current debate on errors in medicine, it is already becoming clear that order entry is only a small component of what must be automated to improve the safety of medication administration.[2] The refinement of an IT system's business logic can only be achieved in the application of a system, preferably in a number of different healthcare settings, including large and small institutions, inpatient and outpatient facilities, academic and community institutions, and so forth. The need to understand what you are automating before you try to automate it is axiomatic.

However, many companies and healthcare organizations are still ignoring the fundamental hard work and experience that must be included for any CPOE system to be both safe and successful. To avoid this pitfall, the reader is encouraged to consider that business logic is the real asset purchased with an established CPOE vendors system, rather than the programming tools or technology. Further, for those brave souls who still endeavor to build the better mousetrap, they should know that there are no technological shortcuts to grasping and codifying the important knowledge and functional networks that make up healthcare delivery. Be prepared for the time, testing, and effort needed to implement systems that enhance rather than disconnect or bypass the human safety nets that have developed in health-care delivery systems over the past 100 years.[3]

INSTALL CPOE WHILE YOU SLEEP!

In our current ATM generation, there is a general consensus that the one thing we all have the least of is time. The rapid growth of the Internet and the reality that moving from 300 baud modems to broadband home access in 20 years has truly changed the lives of many people on the planet (regardless of which side of the digital divide they stand on) has encouraged the development of this new pitfall and accelerated its incidence.

Warning Signs

This pitfall can be termed the "impatient implementer." That is, when an organization believes that a CPOE system is "just another computer system," there is usually a crushing disappointment that can be anticipated within the next 12 to 18 months. The industry is at least partly to blame in that the techno hype of the last decade has encouraged the development of expectations that training is not required and that CPOE systems can be completely implemented out of the box with minimal or no configuration. The fundamental error of this pitfall is a lack of appreciation of both the complexity of the network of processes being automated by CPOE as well as the human factor. By human factor we mean human beings' fundamental inertia to change in any situation. As the debate on both the cost and safety of healthcare is illustrating, American healthcare, while embracing some of the most advanced technologies known, (e.g., genomics) is rooted in institutions that have remained unchanged for centuries (e.g., the physician-patient relationship). Why is it any surprise, therefore, that projects targeting major change in these institutions has resulted in resistance and, even in the best cases, slowness to change?

Cures

Although improvements in adult education and methodologies of transitioning from paper to paperless CPOE environments is aiding in the total time necessary to implement these systems, the need for analysis, communication, and measured evaluation of CPOE project implementation remain key but time consuming requirements of successful projects. Hence the remedy for this pitfall is astute project planning and expectation setting for CPOE proposals.

An additional rule of thumb is that time to complete implementation of CPOE is not linearly related to the size of an organization or health system; rather, it's geometric. The recently reported successful implementation at the Ohio State University (OSU) taking over nine years from planning to execution provides good support for this rule.[4]

THIS TECHNOLOGY IS THE ANSWER, MAN!

Gadgets are everywhere! One of the most amusing and interesting phenomena of dawning years of this century is the spectacle of the technically sophisticated human walking around with a veritable utility belt of technological devices that would make Batman jealous. The plethora of personal digital assistants, polyphone cellular phones, personal Bluetooth-enabled networks, two-way pagers, and more all make it possible for this CPOE pitfall to seduce its victims.

Warning Signs

While we have already discussed the pitfalls of the over-zealous technologist above, this particular pitfall is a bit more subtle but no less threatening, due mainly to its pervasiveness. That is, it will probably be impossible in the remainder of this decade to pull together a CPOE project leadership team without including some individuals who already have a strong technological wish-fulfillment bias. This bias is one of the best allies IT vendor salesmen have ever had. It allows CPOE systems to, as the old ads used to say, "almost sell themselves!" Having had the opportunity of attending numerous sales sessions, we have witnessed CPOE customers selling themselves on systems, projecting features and functions the vendor has never demonstrated or even promised! One of our more cynical colleagues has coined a phrase that illustrates this pitfall: "That system was compiled in PowerPoint®!" to indicate that the demonstrated system exists only in beautifully designed computer images with nary a single line of actual computer code being written.

Cures

The solution to this pervasive technophilia again is management of expectations. Specifically, center your CPOE project group on the key work of understanding tangibles such as project goals, proven functionality, change management and value delivery and measurement. Incorporating the latest usable technologies to improve the interest in and acceptability of CPOE systems is nevertheless a key strategy. For example, the integration of PDAs, wireless networks, data input alternative devices (e.g., voice, writing) can all be considered as enhancements to a CPOE project, without overshadowing the project's overall goals.

CPOE AS SHERMAN'S MARCH TO THE SEA

In 1864, Union General WT Sherman conducted one of the most brutal but successful campaigns of the Civil War. His irresistible drive through the Confederacy is, unfortunately, sometimes emulated metaphorically in this CPOE implementation pitfall. The scenario can be considered the backlash to the history of CPOE implementation in this country as it embodies three elements: (1) technological rigidity; (2) vertical control model for organizational change; and (3) implementation as the over-arching project goal.

While the third element should be considered laudable, the other two embody fundamental errors in understanding the CPOE change management that ultimately result in project failure.

Warning Signs

The best examples of this pitfall are the *one size fits all* clinical system implementations. These strategies usually are applied in a healthcare system in an effort to control costs and time to delivery. What the approach ignores, however, is the need for organization learning and ownership of a core information system like CPOE. Although it is axiomatic to consider CPOE fundamental to healthcare delivery, overly rigid systems, truncated implementation timelines, and attitudes that amount to "slam it in" ultimately result in system rejection and grass roots rebellion to systems.

Due to the cost-constrained environment of American healthcare, examples of systems experiencing this particular pitfall can always be identified when direct physician utilization of a CPOE is replaced by clerical scribing. The added costs of having nurses, clerks, or scribes use the CPOE system essentially consigns the project to a slow death, as the benefits of decision support delivered to the wrong members of the healthcare team reliably fail to achieve the hoped-for improvements in care at the point of service.

Cures
The solutions to this pitfall include (1) incorporation of realistic timelines from the outset of the CPOE project; (2) enlightened and consistent project management providing a balance to necessary CPOE system configuration and customization; and (3) regular and effective communication of the realities and tradeoffs between system implementation delay and feature enhancement requests.

CONTROLLING YOUR MEDICAL STAFF IS EASY!
When veterans of CPOE system implementation gather, one some-times hears nostalgia for an era when medical staff voluntarism could be achieved with an evening of pizza and a slide show. Whether this era ever really existed is a matter of opinion; however, this pitfall is one of the most significant and is responsible for a good deal of the painfully slow growth of CPOE systems in America.

Warning Signs
Risk factors for this pitfall can be demonstrated by several scenarios: (1) post hoc medical staff involvement in the CPOE project; (2) the goal of CPOE project leadership is physician buy-in rather than inte-gration of physician leadership into project decision making and direction; and (3) mandatory physician CPOE use is announced with-out successful communication of the value of direct physician use.

Post hoc physician involvement remains surprisingly common and is a prime reason for staff indifference and lack of ownership of CPOE projects. Interestingly, because physicians are one of the groups most profoundly affected by the introduction of CPOE systems, the history of how a CPOE project came to be and who was involved remain in staff memory for many years longer—unfortunately, some-times longer than the CPOE system project itself!

Cures

Clearly, the solution to this element of the pitfall is communication and involvement of recognized medical staff leadership at the earliest possible time in a CPOE project. Even if system selection has already been narrowed to a few, it will pay dividends for years to come if the physician staff participates in the final culling of choices for the system that they inevitably will need to use and own. We have previously discussed the complexity of the healthcare system workflow that is impacted by CPOE systems. It should come as no surprise, therefore, that the need for in-depth understanding by the medical staff of the values, limitations, and needs for physicians' direct use of these systems is paramount to achieving the promised system benefits for all users.

Thus, the notion of buy-in implying near passive acquiescence is inappropriate when discussing these goals. Rather, medical staff involvement, even championing of CPOE project creation and success, should be the broadly communicated goal from a project's inception. Anything less sends the wrong message to the staff and the organization at large and will ultimately culminate in lack of resilience and staff ownership of the pain of system implementation when the full impact of changes necessary to absorb a CPOE implementation are finally realized.

References

1. See www.digitaldividenetwork.org.
2. Anderson JG, Jay SJ, Anderson M, et al. Evaluating the capability of information technology to prevent adverse drug events: a computer simulation approach. *J Am Med Inform Assoc.* 2002, 9(5):479–490.
3. Patterson ES, Cook RI, Render ML. Improving patient safety by identifying side effects from introducing bar coding in medication administration. *J Am Med Inform Assoc.* 2002, 9:540–553.
4. Ahmad A, Teater P, Bentley TD, et al. Key attributes of a successful physician order entry system implementation in a multi-hospital environment. *J Am Med Inform Assoc.* 2002, 9(1):16–24.

CHAPTER 3

Selling the Value of Automation in Healthcare: Truth Telling and Snake Oil

There is little doubt now that online access to health information is here to stay. However, as with many other aspects of communication and commerce on the Web, the growth has been chaotic and over-hyped. The outcome has revealed several key truths about human communication and illustrated the expectations that both physicians and patients have held about the nature of their relationship.

Some excellent studies of physician-patient communication via e-mail have confirmed that there is indeed a growing segment of the population that is willing and interested in using electronic communication for healthcare interchange. Most important, however, is the strong desire demonstrated by patients to have more timely and convenient access to their physicians. Studies repeatedly have shown that patients mistrust medical information from sources unfamiliar to them, especially when important decisions must be made.[1] However, it has also become clear that the initial enthusiasm patients have had with using e-mail was based on enhanced convenience at interacting with physicians, enabling them to cut across the reality of on-call services, covering physicians, large group practices, and other realities of the modern American cost-managed care environment. It comes as no surprise, therefore, that studies based upon direct access by patients to their recognized physician garnered high satisfaction from patients.[2]

Physicians' reactions to e-mail have been mixed; they include numerous concerns about additional time spent online, lack of reimbursement for services delivered by e-mail, and finally, concerns about "security" of online diagnosis and therapy. We place "security" in quotes because, after closer examination, these concerns are largely based on medical liability and financial reimbursement issues rather than true computer security concerns.

Some large healthcare delivery systems have approached this conundrum by promoting alternatives to unstructured physician-patient e-mail, in the hopes of controlling the interaction as well as addressing administrative issues such as authentication and true security. Although early studies have been generally positive,[3] and indeed some early standards have been proposed for the appropriate structure of online physician-patient communications, many questions remain about the real role or niche that online communications will hold in the delivery of healthcare in this country.

In a recent survey of 60,000 U.S. households, although 40 percent of self-reported patients indicated they sought online healthcare information, only 4 to 6 percent admitted to using e-mail to contact a physician or other health care professional.[4] Therefore the physician-patient online telecare debate goes on, still leaving abundant room for reports from breathless technology enthusiasts that the vast majority of the population will only read but watch with interest, for now.

More importantly, the fact that the dot-com boom went bust is yet another incentive for the conservative healthcare industry, and physicians in particular, to slow their adoption of information technology, feeding the conundrum.

THE SAFETY DEBATE

The safety debate is another arena where excess enthusiasm for technological solutions can foster the physician-computer conundrum. A recent article in the *New England Journal of Medicine* by two residents on the topic of error reduction illustrates perhaps the proper perspective technology holds even for young doctors in the safety debate.[5] Rather than debate the veracity of estimates of excess deaths from medical errors in U.S. hospitals, these authors accept that there is a problem but creatively suggest a number of issues that may result in excess medical errors that do not include computerized provider order entry (CPOE)—and indeed might even have been worsened by the use of technology! Their list of issues includes

1. Frequent interruptions with paging;
2. Orders and medical records (CPOE and CPR);
3. Sign-out procedures;
4. Hours of work;
5. Location of medical charts and equipment;
6. Reporting of errors;
7. Training in procedures; and
8. Leadership.

Although items 2 and 3 came out strongly in support of technological solutions to current problems (e.g., CPOE and automated sign-out systems), one of the items, frequent paging, is a *result* of wireless technology, effecting far too frequent interruptions in the daily work of residents (and of course attending physicians). Therefore, although physicians' enthusiasm for technology has not waned in the first part of the new millennium, physicians are already aware that technology is not *the key or perhaps even the most important* solution to the many problems and issues that result in increased errors in American healthcare today.

Having said this, one of the strongest themes from *To Err is Human* that is rarely discussed in the context of a technological problem is the need to develop a culture of safety in healthcare.[6] That culture change will obviously *require* technology not only to effect improvements in quality (CPOE with decision support, for example) but also to collect data on the important issue of exactly *where* errors are occurring in a particular healthcare system, avoiding the tyranny of controls being placed on healthcare across the board even in situations where no problems exist.

Recognition that the most common method of identifying errors in medicine, self-reporting, is completely inadequate *and* that technology may indeed be useful was reviewed in a recent article in detecting adverse events using information technology.[7] The authors discuss the fact that spontaneous reporting detects the minority of adverse events, dooming *correcting* interventions, technological or otherwise, to either being too many or too few from the outset. The article suggests instead that in using technologies such as event monitoring and natural language processing, there has been a sufficient body of study showing that better event detection (such as adverse drug events and nosocomial infections) can result, thereby enabling *targeted* interventions for improvement in safety where they really are needed.

DRIVERS FOR CHANGE

Over the years there have been many greatly anticipated drivers for the dissemination of information technology into the country's healthcare. For example, when mainframe technology began to give way to client-server technology with its improved user interfaces, there was excitement that this would help move clinicians to using computers in the daily practice of medicine. The PC and Internet technologies offered similar hopes, mostly unrealized.

As healthcare information standards (e.g., HL7) were introduced, these too were hoped to be the key "push" that would transform the industry. Unfortunately, with few exceptions, these technological trends failed to alter the rate of growth of information technology in healthcare.

In 2000 the Institute of Medicine (IOM) published the seminal work, *To Err is Human,* which addressed concerns of quality and safety in the American healthcare system in a sensational way, directly targeting *systems'* role in improving safety. Although there have been innumerable articles contesting the magnitude of the problem identified by the IOM, there is no question that the work has generated an abiding concern and action in this country attempting to identify and implement improved safety systems into healthcare.

One of the first signs that the IOM publication was having a meaningful effect was the development of the Leapfrog Group (www.leapfroggroup.org). This consortium of payers, insurers, providers, and industry leaders in healthcare moved the discussion forward by stating that they were convinced of the importance of the healthcare problems that the IOM identified, and further that they were prepared to be even more specific in recommending changes to the healthcare industry. One of these recommendations included encouraging the use of computerized physician order entry. In addition, the Leapfrog Group suggested that although they were starting with recommendations, in the future, patients employed by member organizations would be encouraged to patronize systems that had embraced their recommendations. Although in subsequent publications the Leapfrog Group has softened its tone as well as clarified that the group was not going to actually subsidize the acquisition of the IT necessary to come into compliance with its recommendations, its first bold step was not the first shot across the bow of technological complacency in modern healthcare.

In a recent study from Kaiser/Harvard School of Public Health, 831 physicians and 1,207 nonphysician adults were surveyed regarding what they believed to be the actual causes of errors in medical care.[8] Physicians blamed nursing shortages (53 percent) and overworked, stressed, or fatigued health care workers (50 percent). The nonphysician adults polled blamed

1. Physicians not having enough time with patients (72 percent);
2. Overworked, stressed or fatigued healthcare workers (70 percent);
3. Healthcare workers not working or communicating as a team (67 percent); and
4. Nursing shortages (65 percent).

The authors concluded, "Physicians disagree with national experts on the effectiveness of many of the proposed solutions to the problem of medical errors." (See further discussion of this study later in this chapter.)

Despite these disagreements, there continue to be efforts to align incentives in the healthcare field to promote the adoption and use of clinical information systems. On July 8, 2002, New York's Empire Blue Cross (www.empireblue.com) began making bonus payments to hospitals if those hospitals used, or will use, CPOE. The quarterly 4 percent bonus payments are part of an experiment by companies that are partners in the Leapfrog Group. Then incentive will decline annually to 2 percent in 2004. Similar experiments are being proposed in California and Wisconsin (http://www.ahrq.gov/clinic/ptsafety/).

In sum, therefore, the national dialog, residing the crest of the "errors in medicine" wave, is showing more and more meaningful activity inching towards a national agenda for implementing information technology in the healthcare industry. However, progress remains tentative and slow. The key—convincing two of the most important groups of the need for change, patients and physicians—has not yet occurred. Therefore, it is clear that although in the future this agenda will truly change the face of healthcare's automation scene, much convincing still needs to be done.

Defining the key milestones that need to be met to truly catalyze and accelerate this change are the topic of innumerable discussions in the industry, but they boil down to five issues:

1. Standardization of technology solutions (the continued plethora of CPOE systems with incompatible databases, communication/ interface strategies and user interfaces continue to support the sarcastic adage: "If you've seen one clinical information system, you've seen one;"

2. There must be a consensus within the medical profession that, for the practice of state of the art care, information systems are a *requirement;*

3. The cost of implementing systems, both capital and operational, and the time required for system configuration and training, must fall substantially to allow widespread dissemination in a healthcare industry already growing at a rate alarming to American society at large;

4. There need to be more clinical *experts* in the configuration and implementation of CPOE systems, better enabling rapid, cost effective, and successful CPOE system implementation; and finally

5. Healthcare organization leadership must have clear, binding incentives, aligned with physicians and IT vendors to achieve efficient, effective acquisition and implementation of CPOE in their organizations.

ALIGNMENT OF INCENTIVES

This latter point—alignment of incentives—warrants further elucidation. To describe the key incentives needed, let us examine three key groups in this equation: (1) healthcare system leadership; (2) physicians; and (3) CPOE vendors.

Healthcare System Leadership

By healthcare system leadership we mean the so-called "C-Suite": CIO, CEO, CFO, COO. The incentives necessary to motivate this group to select and implement CPOE systems must be in one or more of the following categories:

1. Regulatory incentives, e.g., JCAHO review and accreditation requirements;
2. Business incentives, including competitive market forces;
3. Financial incentives, e.g., planned ROI eliminating operating costs by automation (e.g., the paperless medical records department); and/or
4. Litigation avoidance incentives (e.g., improvement in quality and reduction of medical errors).

Physicians

For physicians to have incentives to adopt CPOE systems, several recent articles describe the importance of financial incentives to the broad acceptance of computerized systems in physician practice. A report in the *British Medical Journal* describes an interesting situation in the National Health System (NHS) in Great Britain, where extremely high use of information systems by primary care physicians has been achieved (greater than 90 percent), while to the present day, fewer than 15 percent of hospital-based physicians use CPOE or other clinical information systems in daily practice.[9] The author concludes that financial incentives (low cost or free hardware, actual financial incentives) provided to community physicians and no consistent complementary policy for in-hospital physicians is the determining factor. The story of the Department of Veterans Affairs (VA) system in the United States, however, provides another example of where broad implementation of CPOE and standardization of systems provide such a compelling improvement in a healthcare network that physicians adopt systems even without direct financial incentives.

Although financial incentives for physicians are paramount, several other factors are important for physician adoption: (1) compelling literature demonstrating the value of such systems (e.g., reduction in errors, improvement in efficiency of practice with systems); (2) adequate system flexibility supporting the necessary variation in physician practice; and (3) patient interest and support for CPOE systems. All three of the latter incentive trends are in play in the United States but are, as of this publication, at surprisingly early stages. Physicians need compelling data showing the value of implementation and use of CPOE systems as well as honest, accurate information on impact on their income and time in learning and using CPOE systems.

Nevertheless, we must conclude that in the current state of U.S. healthcare and the medical profession, without direct financial incentives for physicians to adopt and effectively use CPOE systems, all of the previously mentioned incentives will be inadequate to overcome the inertia in system propagation that has plagued this country's healthcare scene for over 35 years.

CPOE Vendors

Vendors of CPOE systems currently suffer from a plethora of problems that must be overcome to provide the proper incentive alignment with healthcare leadership and physician groups. The key elements requiring resolution are

1. Technology standardization;
2. Decreased development costs;
3. Simplified implementation strategies allowing more rapid market growth;
4. Business change so that differentiation can occur without propagating the current nightmare of proprietary system interfacing; and
5. Improved strategies of migration of existing client base to the current technologies.

The importance of this redefinition of the CPOE vendor business can have no better demonstration than the VA system's adoption of the computer-based patient record system (CPRS) throughout the country. While the VA system has required many years to accomplish its impressive feat, the national network of VA hospitals now has a consistent technological platform, the ability of sharing enhancements to system function across the country due to product standardization, and such futuristic capabilities as complete electronic charting and data transfers to and from any VA hospital in the country.

Many factors helped achieve the success that is evident in this system today, such as

- Technology choices were limited;
- Decisions on achieving implementation were centrally mandated;
- The mandate that "failure is not an option" was made clear to all involved from the outset;
- Different VA hospitals were allowed to set their own timetables for system introduction; and
- In many VA hospitals, young physicians in training (interns/residents) make up the bulk of the ordering physician work force.

However, the key lesson from the VA experience for CPOE vendors at the end of the day may be standardization. The long running joke in healthcare IT goes like this: "We love standards in IT because we have so many of them!" In 2004 this joke now appears more like gallows humor as vendors who have acquired a plethora of competitors struggle both to understand and reconcile disparate platforms and technologies and become completely unable to demonstrate seamless integration of systems even within their own product line! The era of when "Single Source Vendor" decisions would surely result in a functional CPOE environment is over. Although rapid technology changes are at least partially responsible for this quandary, the rapid healthcare IT acquisition frenzy of the 1990s is where most of the responsibility lies.

For CPOE vendors, standardization would need to become a tool to achieve two major goals for better incentive alignment: decreased cost of system development and decreased cost of legacy system migration and integration.

This warrants some further explanation. Current healthcare IT vendors have had to differentiate their products on several bases:

1. Functionality;
2. Purported technology superiority;
3. Graphic user environment;
4. Ease of use; and
5. Cost.

Unfortunately, the byproduct of having functionality as a key differentiator has been the evolution of proprietary, nonstandards-based programming. This proprietary programming/technology more easily supports both the legal and economic protection of the product assets of a company. However, what it achieves for the users of these systems is a virtual "electronic tower of Babel" that has likely resulted in more failed CPOE and other healthcare IT projects than any other single factor.

But how could this situation ever be changed? Isn't it hopeless? Again, the VA system holds a lesson for us here. Although we have emphasized the importance of standardization among the hospitals in the VA system, there are definitely projects expanding on the basic CPOE system that differentiate single VA hospitals around the country. These examples suggest that commercial standardization could be accomplished by federal legislation mandating technology standards as the basis for system development. The argument could be made that this fundamental standardization is necessary to better ensure the safety and quality of these systems in healthcare throughout the country. However, healthcare vendors could then be encouraged to differentiate functionality and product based upon enhancements on the basic system. In fact, if standardization for fundamental technology could be achieved in healthcare IT, vendors would be able to achieve lower development costs and easier legacy migration and interfacing/support. This would also permit a far more enlightened development environment encouraging true innovation instead of endlessly recreating code to perform *exactly* the same functions on different application platforms. (How many different ways do we need to transmit an order from a nursing station to a pharmacy?)

In the national discourse on errors in medicine, there may be a secret ally appearing in this need for standardization: That vendors will need to be held to explicit standards of code quality and system performance in real world settings. Only with fewer vendors, programming standards, and much larger market shares could this kind of change occur in the current CPOE vendor environment. The national errors debate, therefore, may hold the key answers to our current conundrum.

The Value of Automation

Are we making progress? In December 2002 the *Washington Post* reported that little had been done to reduce death and injury from medical errors as the November 29, 1999 IOM report had urged.[10] The article noted that although the report generated a good deal of activity, little progress has been made. This was despite the introduction of four bills on Capitol Hill, the creation of a consortium of Fortune 500 companies in 2000 to press hospitals to make specific changes in operations including the adoption of CPOE systems, and wide coverage in the press.

Although medical errors, wrong-site surgery, hospital-acquired infections, house officer fatigue, and poor supervision and the nursing shortage were all cited as contributing to the high risk of errors in U.S. healthcare, it is the first factor—medical errors—that appears the best documented, with the best studied solution that remains the most vexing. The *Washington Post* article pointed out that although the IOM's conclusion that as many as 98,000 hospitalized Americans die every year and 1 million more are injured as a result of preventable medical errors that cost the nation an estimated $29 billion, only a handful (2 percent) of American hospitals have IT systems in place and, with the exception of the VA medical system, most have not taken steps necessary to protect patients from errors. Reasons for this failure are not entirely clear but seem to include the following elements:

1. Lack of a transparent error reporting system in American medicine;
2. Absence of substantial financial incentives (litigation costs exempted) for hospitals/health system compliance with error reduction measures;
3. Physician resistance to error recognition and reporting;
4. Costly and poorly functioning healthcare IT systems; and
5. At the end of the day, society's general indifference to the matter of errors in healthcare as a whole.

Still, this report concludes that some progress is being made, for example, the new JCAHO regulatory changes addressing some specific error-prone behaviors that went into effect January 2003. There is little doubt that the magnitude of the problem of serious errors in American healthcare still is not known, and that as a society, we will need to decide soon if we want to remedy the situation.

Although there are many who consider the data surrounding the decrease in medical errors with use of information technology compelling, there is a growing literature for the skepticism of our society at large as to the value of CPOE and other IT in healthcare. First Health Group reported on a survey of 1,002 Americans 18 years of age or older from the general population about their opinions regarding the use of IT to manage health.[11] They reported that 53 percent of respondents believed that new information technology will end up being more trouble than doing things the old way, 77 percent believed that doctors would miss subtle clues in online interactions that would be picked up normally in face to face visits, 60 percent were concerned that technology would replace much in-person care, driving doctors even further from their patients, 61 percent believed that new technologies would raise the cost of healthcare and 89 percent believed the patient would end up paying that cost.

On the positive side, both Internet-enabled monitoring and personalized management via e-mail or telephone were felt by the majority to potentially improve care and provide them with a sense of control and empowerment in managing their health. If supported by further studies, it is clear that further proof of efficacy and value for dollars spent will be needed before synergy between concern for reduction in medical errors and seeking the use of IT solutions will be supported by the general public.

One concern in the skepticism about the value of automation in modern healthcare was cited in an article in the American Psychological Association *Monitor* (APAM) emphasizing that once we rely on automation, we are placed in a monitoring role, a role for which we are ill-suited.[12] The authors suggested that automated systems need to be developed that do not simply replace human functions, but rather provide *adaptive automation,* that is, a system that changes its functioning in response to how the human operator(s) is working. In this way, the human operator remains engaged in the decision making process rather than being lulled into complacency, merely accepting the output of the automation. The reality of the fallibility of even systems specifically designed for pharmaceutical monitoring has been reported lending credence to these concerns.[13] The experience of many healthcare IT leaders on implementation of CPOE alerts is very much in keeping with the APAM report, suggesting that although we are making progress with our system's ability to provide decision support, we may need yet more sophisticated technology to really do the job properly.

Sometimes data reporting can achieve desired alignment of incentives in healthcare significantly improving outcomes. As reported in *American Medical News,* the Tri-River Healthcare Coalition in Dayton, Ohio, reported the results of community wide efforts to improve death rates due to heart attacks through an information based strategy involving employers, physicians, and health systems. Over a three-year period heart attack deaths decreased by 36 percent in this community.[14] The necessary interventions involved a truly across the board analysis and targeted interventions including emergency services, care protocols, and even the threat of publishing hospital outcome data. Although the latter threat was never acted upon, participants agreed that it provided one of the key drivers for increasing competition between hospitals and practitioners that led to the beneficial changes.

A new computer networked that collected and distributed information was key to the success. The rapid turnaround of data was felt to be important to the final outcome as it provided timely information that all groups could act upon since, as the director of clinical management at participating Kettering Medical Center noted, "... You can't get data a year and a half later and expect to do much with it. If you get data in a rapid fashion, you can look at care issues instead of just outcomes."

It is hard to overestimate this power of *data at hand.* In considering the current state of managed care in America, one might consider its failure as a matter of data availability. That is, since we didn't have readily available clinical information such as electronic medical records (EMR) as managed care arose in the 1990s, but rather readily available financial information, that is what organizations used. The focus was placed on cost, ultimately managing a *surrogate* of the healthcare process, charges, rather than the actual process itself. How could the outcome be anything other than restricting access to care from this fundamental error?

MOMENTUM FOR REDUCING MEDICAL ERRORS

So the IOM, the Leapfrog Group, and the American Medical Association (AMA) have sounded the alarm about errors in medical care in the United States and clearly stated that computer systems (CPOE in particular) are important solutions to the problem. That was in 1999. However the rate of EMR use over the last decade hasn't changed from the reported 5–10 percent. So why haven't we come a longer way?

An important wakeup call for the healthcare IT industry was delivered in the December 12, 2002, issue of the *New England Journal of Medicine* when Robert Blendon and colleagues at the Harvard School of Public Health reported on a survey on the prevailing opinions of errors in medicine from both a large physician and public cohort.[15] They conducted parallel randomized national surveys of 831 practicing physicians and 1,207 members of the public asking the following questions:

1. Have you had a personal experience with medical errors made in your care or that of a family member?
2. How frequent and how serious is the problem of medical errors as compared with other problems in healthcare?
3. What are the most important causes of medical errors?
4. What actions should be taken to prevent medical errors? and
5. What should be the consequences for a health professional or institution involved in a medical error?

The answers to these questions have provided a fascinating insight into what may be the most important reasons our healthcare and society have accepted neither the urgency of errors and medicine nor the adoption of CPOE and other automation technologies in our country: *We don't believe it!*

This is not to say the respondents in this survey had not been touched by medical errors. Thirty-five percent of physicians and 42 percent of the public reported that they had experienced an error in their own care or that of a family member, including 18 percent of physicians and 24 percent of the public reporting an error that resulted in serious consequences including death. Disturbingly 29 percent of physicians reported having seen an error in the previous year and 60 percent believed that a similar error was very or somewhat like to occur during the next year.

However, neither physicians nor the public named medical errors as one of the largest problems in healthcare today. The physicians believed the costs of malpractice insurance, lawsuits, the cost of healthcare, and problems with insurance companies and health plans were the paramount issues. In the survey of the public the top problems were noted as cost of healthcare and the cost of prescription drugs. Only 5 percent of physicians and 6 percent of the public identified medical errors as one of the most serious problems. Both groups' estimates of serious medical errors per year were also far less than the estimate published by the IOM (5,000 per year compared to 98,000 per year).

What of the use of information systems as the proper way to deal with errors? The bad news is that only 23 percent of physicians believed that CPOE would be the way to decrease the problem of medical errors, and that 19 percent believed medical errors would decrease if use of computerized patient records (CPR) was an option. The public was only slightly more enthusiastic, picking CPOE 45 percent of the time and CPR 46 percent of the time. Rather, physicians believed that requiring hospitals to develop systems for preventing errors or increasing the numbers of nurses were more important. The public rated the following four items as effective steps toward reducing errors: spending more time with patients; requiring hospitals to develop systems for preventing errors; providing better training of health professionals; and using only physician trained in intensive care medicine on ICUs.

A CREDIBILITY GAP

The authors of this Harvard study concluded "*The momentum for instituting changes to reduce medical errors is sustained primarily by a range of groups and by the media's interest in the problem—not by practicing physicians or the public.*" It seems clear that if this study is representative of physicians and the American public, the publications of the IOM, the Leapfrog Group, and media coverage notwithstanding, there is a serious credibility gap in belief even in the *existence* of a crisis in errors in medicine, much less the urgency to rapidly move forward with automation in healthcare. We have our work cut out for us!

Understanding of this credibility gap is advanced by a report in the *Journal of Family Practice* by Dr. Glenn Loomis and colleagues entitled "*If electronic medical records are so great, why aren't family physicians using them?. . ."*[16] This survey of 618 Indiana family practitioners revealed that only 14.4 percent currently used an EMR. Unsurprisingly, only half of nonusers believed that current EMRs are useful for physicians. However, the vast majority of EMR users and nonusers in this primarily ambulatory care practice setting (more than 80 percent) believed systems are far too costly. Further, the authors report that only 55 percent of EMR users and 13.4 percent of nonusers believe data entry is easy for current EMRs. In what might be considered the last straw for beleaguered community physicians, the majority of surveyed non-EMR-user physicians believed that paper records were more secure than EMRs despite available literature. Lest the reader believe the surveyed physicians were Luddites, 93 percent reported using computers, 67 percent currently used the Internet, and 30 percent used PDAs in their practice. Therefore, besides the dissonance on the medical error issue, primary care in early years of this century still seem to have more reasons to wait and see rather than embrace and make effective use of automation in medical practice.

Are informaticians and the American public (physicians and the public at large) talking past one another in this matter? An excellent article by Dr. Daniel R. Masys entitled *Effects of Current and Future Information Technologies on the Health Care Workforce* illustrated the striking polarity of debate as the author described what is nothing less than the imminent transformation of healthcare and the medical profession in this era of the Internet and genomics.[17] For example, Masys quoted the growth of the National Library of Medicine (NLM) Medline database as 400,000 new entries per year on an existing base of 11.7 million citations. A tongue in cheek calculation shows that if a physician reads two articles every evening, at the end of the year he/she will be approximately 550 years behind in keeping up with the literature! Furthermore, the growing domain of genomics, an entirely new dimension to the delivery of medicine that is intensely data driven, is now appearing, making the traditional model of autonomous, human memory-dependent practice an endangered behavior at best.

We recognize that although scientific data have demonstrated the value of incorporation of information technology into the daily practice of medicine, the value has not yet become compelling. The social and political reality is that not only do the major stakeholder groups remain skeptical, but they believe that for whatever value automation may have in healthcare, it's too expensive and may be more worrisome from a security/privacy standpoint, and there are many other changes that need to be made to American healthcare first.

There can be little doubt that only by a comprehensive approach to this physician-computer conundrum (and what may be called the public-computer conundrum as well) can we hope to make progress towards the introduction of the systems needed to improve American healthcare. This approach will need at a minimum several key elements:

1. Continued credible research addressing the real concerns of the stakeholder groups;
2. Development of better CPOE systems answering both the ease of use and cost concerns;
3. Continued efforts at education for all parties, healthcare leadership, physicians and the public; and
4. Time.

Why time? Consider *time* another way of saying *evolution*. In 1992 we wrote *The Physician-Computer Connection* endeavoring to encourage budding leaders in clinical IT to take up the challenge of direct physician use information system. In 2004 we are publishing this work, *The Physician-Computer Conundrum*, a treatise analyzing why more progress hasn't been made in this field to date and proposing solutions and approaches to facilitate the migration. In the future we may release *The Physician-Computer Collision!* This is only slightly tongue in cheek. Consider this: We are now educating new physicians at the threshold of an entirely new era of medicine, genomics. This cohort of physicians will *out of necessity* be highly computer savvy, navigating multidimensional databases as a necessary aspect of their profession. There will be *no* expectation of retaining all one needs to know in long-term memory, rather, the skills necessary to know what systems to have at ones fingertips and how to use them in the daily practice of medicine, will become the standard practice.

If you are in a teaching institution, look around. Note how many new interns are loaded down with the *Washington Manual* as we were, compared to those toting around a PDA or accessing information just-in-time online. Now as this new generation begins to take over the power structure of medical hierarchy, are U.S. healthcare institutions going to get away with handing them incomplete paper charts, shipping them lab, radiology, and other reports weeks or months after ordering them? *A collision is inevitable!* Therefore, we believe that if current trends in medical information and education continue, there will not only be better *acceptance* of healthcare IT infrastructure, it will be *demanded*.

The reader might be tempted to consider that all of this resistance to CPOE might be overcome virtually overnight with federal legislation and Joint Commission regulatory mandates. This would be a matter of *ifs* at the time of this writing. That is, *If* the aforementioned recent studies of both public and physician opinions on the value of CPOE/EMRs are *not* representative of those populations, *If* the necessary financial support necessary to achieve a broad-based implementation of CPOE/EMR systems throughout the country became available, *If* the political lobby power of big business were to identify the acquisition and implementation of these systems as a top priority, and finally, *If* issues of healthcare access and cost were to be overcome in the near-term, *Then* the legislative/regulatory solution would hold promise for success.

Otherwise, as the post-9/11 world has taught us, there are far too many other concerns in our world to promote this controversial agenda to an easy or safe political win.

References

1. Kane B, Sands DZ. Guidelines for the clinical use of electronic mail with patients. The AMIA Internet working group, task force on guidelines for the use of clinic-patient electronic mail. *J Am Med Inform Assoc.* 1998, 5(1):104–111.
2. Liederman EM, Morefield CS. Web messaging: a new tool for patient-physician communication. *J Am Med Inform Assoc.* 2003, 10:260–270.
3. Sittig DF, King S, Hazlehurst BL. A survey of patient-provider e-mail communication: what do patients think? *Int J Med Inf.* 2001, 61(1):71–80.
4. Baker L, Wagner TH, Singer S, Bundorf MK. Use of the Internet and e-mail for health care information: results from a national survey. *JAMA.* 2003, 189:400–406.
5. Volpp KGM, Grande D. Residents' suggestions for reducing errors in teaching hospitals. *N Engl J Med.* 2003, 348:851–855.
6. Kohn LT, Corrigan JM, Donaldson MS, eds. *To Err Is Human: Building a Safer Health System.* Institute of Medicine, Committee on Quality of Health Care in America. Washington, DC: National Academy Press, 2000.
7. Bates DW, Evans RS, Murff H, et al. Detecting adverse events using information technology. *J Am Med Inform Assoc.* 2003, 10:115–128.

8. Blendon RJ, DesRoches CM, Brodie M, et al. Patient safety: views of practicing physicians and the public on medical errors. *N Engl J Med.* 2002, 347:1933–1940.

9. Benson T. Why general practitioners use computers and hospital doctors do not. Part 1: incentives. *BMJ.* 2002, 325:1086–1089.

10. Boodman SG. *Washington Post.* December 3, 2002. www.washingtonpost.com.

11. www.firsthealth.com, February 23, 2002.

12. Azar B. Danger of automation: it makes us complacent. *APA Monitor.* 29: July, 1998.

13. Institute for Safe Medical Practices Medication Safety Alert. February 10, 1999.

14. *American Medical News.* December 16, 2002.

15. Blendon RJ, DesRoches CM, Brodie M, et al. Views of practicing physicians and the public on medical errors. *N Engl J Med.* 2002, 347:1933–1940.

16. Loomis GA, Ries JS, Saywell RM Jr, et al. If electronic medical records are so great, why aren't family physicians using them? *J Fam Pract.* 2002, 51(7).

17. Masys DR. Effects of current and future information technologies on the health care workforce. *Health Affairs.* 2002, 21(5):33–41.

CHAPTER 4

Examples from the Front Lines

In the real world of healthcare IT, groups endeavoring to replicate successes reported elsewhere have been frustrated with the lack of systematic, usable documentation of how the successful organizations did it, and more importantly, how other groups can learn from and transfer these successful practices to their own institutions.

Then in 1994 the Nicholas E Davies CPR (computerized patient records) Recognition Program was created by the Computerized Patient Record Institute (CPRI) to address this issue by recognizing excellence in the practical application of the CPR in healthcare. Established in 1994, the Davies Recognition Program has awarded 19 organizations for implementation of electronic health records (EHR). The program is named after Dr. Nicholas E. Davies who was a practicing physician, president-elect of the American College of Physicians, and a member of the Institute of Medicine (IOM) Committee on Improving the Patient Record when he died in an airplane crash in 1991. Dr. Davies was an accomplished physician who believed that the computer-based patient record was needed to improve patient care.

Over the years, Davies Award winners have provided inspiration to the entire community in achievements proving that it can be done.

This chapter will examine the success of two recent award winners, Maimonides Medical Center (MMC), Brooklyn New York, and Ohio State University (OSU).

MAIMONIDES MEDICAL CENTER

Maimonides Medical Center (MMC) is a not-for-profit, voluntary hospital and the third largest independent teaching hospital in the country. The 705-bed hospital provides care for 36,861 discharges, 77,118 emergency room visits, and 253,316 ambulatory visits. MMC has a staff of 4,612 employees, with 277 staff physicians and 978 community physicians. In 1996 MMC executive management made a commitment for a new information environment with the goals of improving the quality of care, increasing patient satisfaction, reducing costs, and positioning the hospital for growth. Their accomplishment is an excellent example of goals-directed CPR implementation with impressive outcomes.

MMC's computerized patient records system (named the Maimonides Access Clinical System (MACS), comprises four electronic medical records systems (EMRs):

1. Eclipsys 7000 inpatient CPR;
2. NextGen Ambulatory Care CPR;
3. E&C IPRob Perinatal CPR; and
4. A4 Health Systems Emergency Department CPR.

In addition to these institutional systems, there are ten departmental feeder systems including ancillary systems, picture archiving and communications systems (PACS), and decision support systems (DSSs). In 2002 MMC reported 100 percent use of the MACS by all staff including community- and hospital-based physicians. This utilization includes functions of order entry, results reporting, allergy/drug interactions, and concurrent decision support.

Reported benefits of the MACS reads like a wish list for any medical system in the country:

1. 68 percent decrease in medication processing time;
2. 55 percent decrease in medication discrepancies;
3. 58 percent reduction in problem medication orders;
4. 20 percent decrease in duplication of ancillary orders;
5. 48 percent reduction in duplicate lab testing;

6. Over seven years, MACS has contributed to a 2.21 day (30.4 percent) reduction in average length of patient stay; and

7. The improvements accrued as a result of MACS has enabled 32,168 additional inpatients to be served by MMC representing over $50 million in increased revenue, one-fourth of which is attributed to the CPR.

MACS creators identify five key success factors:

1. Establishing programs and methodologies aimed at physician participation and ownership;

2. Building clinically focused MIS staff;

3. Selecting appropriate vendor partners;

4. Conducting training to meet the needs of all user constituencies; and

5. Winning the support of key leaders and advocates.

We will focus on the detail of several elements of their successful journey.

Prior to MACS, Maimonides was entirely mired in what they call, "the punch-card era." The vision needed to begin a transformation as profound as MACS turned out to be had to come from senior leaders. At MMC these were CEO Stanley Brezenoff and COO Pamela Brier. Their vision included the risky but essential commitment to achieving 100 percent physician adoption of CPOE in order to realize the benefits of automation, including improved clinical decision making. An essential step was the clear articulation and broad communication of strategic objectives.

While many organizations use the opportunity of developing strategic objectives for a CPR project as a perfunctory statement of organizational platitudes, MMC thoughtfully and creatively took advantage of the chance to better understand and communicate with their staff. The strategic objectives for the MACS are

1. Improve service efficiency by streamlining healthcare process and workflow to reduce costs and medical errors;

2. Facilitate decision support;

3. Improve patient outcomes;

4. Provide access to patient records and images at remote locations; and

5. Improve patient satisfaction.

Further, they carefully mapped these objectives to the actual systems planned as part of the MACS effort.

MMC identified three leadership factors that were critical to the success of their CPR effort:

1. Strong CEO prepared for expected difficulties, in particular community physician resistance;
2. Financial commitment ($41.8 million) not only for purchase and installation of the CPR but critical elements of training (see below), help desk, and other change management activities;
3. Organizational fortitude in the face of the reality that no other New York City community physician hospital had used a hospital information system.

The inpatient system was purchased in 1992 and implemented in 1996 with continuous system rollouts over the intervening years, in fact continuing to the present time. The MACS is therefore described as a "modified best of breed strategy" as leadership recognized early in the process that no single vendor solution could meet the organization's information needs. We use the term "modified" because MMC, instead of embarking on the selection of a myriad of separate departmental systems purely for the purpose of acquiring the elusive notion of the "best" systems, worked closely with its vendors to develop tailored systems that provided precise functional components that individual departments actually required. In this way the need to deliver the benefits of improved clinical practice were paramount rather than subordinate to technological elitism. Furthermore, MMC made it quite clear that these departmental systems had to comply with the technical standards established by the core institutional systems.

Project governance included specific support for paid clinicians both as part of the core MACS leadership as well as key departmental involvement (e.g., cardiology, obstetrics). This was done in order to both achieve the needed clinical input for system design as well as to enable the lines of clinician communication that can make or break staff acceptance of change in implementing a new CPR.

To their credit, the MACS implementation team adopted an aggressive and comprehensive approach to system training in order to accomplish their goal of 100 percent system use. Four key strategies were used to accomplish MACS training:

1. Training customized to each caregiver segment (e.g., physicians, nurses, ancillary care workers, and so forth);
2. Right training staff (i.e., community physicians were used to learning from staff registered nurses);
3. Right time (e.g., avoiding high census, individually scheduled sessions for busy office physicians, and so forth); and
4. Right training manuals, including a special "MD training guide" designed for the lab coat pocket.

As of March 2002, the MMC staff had conducted more than 61,000 hours of formal training for 13,722 individuals.

Physicians received 3 hours of MACS training, nurses 12 hours. However, MMC cleverly packaged multiple system training so that users would learn Internet and PC skills as well as MACS skills at sessions, providing added value and important educational buttressing for users arriving at all levels of computer literacy.

MMC has thus demonstrated that even in a highly competitive managed care environment such as New York City, a large scale CPR/CPOE implementation can be successfully accomplished by aligning the key elements of

1. Visionary and steadfast top leadership;
2. Laser sharp focus on clinically relevant project goals;
3. Subordination of technological issues to the business and clinical goals of the organization;
4. Substantial investment in a comprehensive training model in recognition of the complexity of the job of patient care and the significance of the change of adopting a complex CPR; and
5. Building success on success, thereby progressively engaging all groups, from early adopters to bulwarks of the establishment, and letting those who have experienced the results of successful implementation do all the talking and convincing of others. Let us examine each of these in light of our road map from Chapter 1.

Visionary and steadfast top leadership: as we discussed in Chapter 1, the implementation of a PCIS is a multiyear endeavor, with benefits accruing mostly at the end of the project—that is, after full implementation. Under these conditions, having a stable, committed (visionary), and unwavering (when the going gets tough, and it will) leadership is absolutely essential. MMC provides a case in point of how this kind of leadership in place can make the difference in achieving success.

Clinically relevant project goals and subordination of technological issues to clinical goals: There's no question about it, the implementation of a PCIS includes an almost irresistible (for the technophilic) component of "gee whiz!" That is, although the value of a PCIS to an organization is essentially tied entirely to the benefits it delivers for the business of clinical medicine, many have been seduced into believing that the implementation of technology was a goal in and of itself. Such projects gone astray are easy to recognize when you hear leadership wax enthusiastic about their success in implementing the latest technology fad, rather than touting how the PCIS has improved their patient care enterprise. The MMC project illustrates how focusing on the clinical process first and foremost (e.g., the decision on the special needs of OB-Gyn) results in success regardless of technology used to reach those goals, provided the technology is proven, reliable and sound.

Training: Education is one of the most commonly quoted reasons for failure of clinician utilization of a PCIS, yet it is the most typical budget component of a PCIS project to be severely trimmed (or eliminated!) when cutting costs on a project. MMC's major investment in both the fundamentals of computer use *and* CPOE-specific education for all clinicians clearly paid off in their implementation. Although marketing talk of intuitive and easy to use systems still goes on, the reality is that the complexity of modern day PCIS systems is such that careful training is essential for success.

Incremental project success: Winning hearts and minds as we discussed in Chapter 1 is illustrated by the project strategy that MMC employed. Their approach of building success on success, and widely communicating and celebrating it, is a winning strategy toward maintaining that all important momentum an organization needs to continue to support and invest in a PCIS.

THE OHIO STATE UNIVERSITY HEALTH SYSTEM

The Ohio State University (OSU) Health System, another Davies Award winner in 2001, another successful CPOE/CPR implementation at a large teaching institution, further expands on which strategies result in success.[1]

OSU focused on three main criteria from the outset of their four year CPOE project as measures of success: (1) system needed to be deployable across diverse clinical environments; (2) it had to focus on physicians as the primary users; and (3) it had to be accepted by clinicians. A telling statement on how the OSU leadership achieved alignment of goals is the fact that they maintained the belief that "Physician order entry is viewed as a logical extension of the OSUHS strategic plan."

Although the authors report a four-year rapid deployment, the total time line (Figure 4-1) reveals a total time line from 1994 through 2001 for completion of their project. Delays caused by Y2K issues and development notwithstanding, this long-term commitment even in the setting of a large academic center, is typical, and it is essential that organizational leadership know about it up front. We say "essential" because the only thing more difficult than initially coming up with the financial support for a CPOE/CPR project is the ability to sustain support for the investment over the many years required for project completion!

The OSU report cites the key strategic factors that enabled physician acceptance of their system as

- Specialty-specific order sets;
- Engagement of physician leadership; and
- Large-scale system implementation.

Specialty-specific order sets are essential to achieve both the benefits of improved ease of use of the CPOE system for physicians and also the key benefit of decreased cost of care, since subspecialty order sets create de facto local standards of care—the ideal means of controlling unnecessary practice variation for quality and cost improvements.

Engagement of physician leadership again reminds us of the lessons of Drs. Jim Andersen and Steve Jay who pointed out almost 20 years ago that to achieve success with CPOE, the informal as well as formal medical leadership must be identified and addressed.[2] Andersen and Jay reported on the adoption of CPOE in a neurology group and the strategies that proved successful. Only when the member of the group who had been a recognized clinical practice leader was convinced of the benefits of using CPOE, did the other members of the group fall in line.

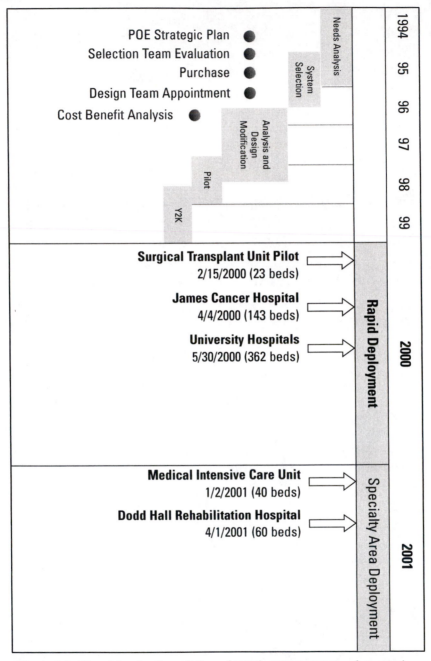

Figure 4-1. Time Line for Completion of OSU's CPOE/CPR Implementation.

(From Ahmad A, Teater P, Bentley TD, et al. Key attributes of a successful physician order entry system implementation in a multi-hospital environment. *J Am Med Inform Assoc.* 2002, 9(1):16–24. Used by permission.)

Large-scale system implementation at OSU meant the avoidance of multiple ordering processes as the system became available throughout this large operation. This key factor addresses the importance of integrated healthcare teams in the modern medical center, and the importance of maintaining intergroup communication, especially at times of change. That the introduction of information technology represents a very profound change is evident. However, a recent report from the VA illustrates how seriously the implementation of a technology, in this case bar coding medication administration, can negatively affect patient care.[3]

CONCLUDING PRECEPTS

In conclusion, the successful implementation of CPOE/CPR systems at MMC and OSU illustrate a number of important precepts worth reviewing. The strategic planning for CPOE must be detailed and organization-specific. Furthermore, the plan must be comprehended and communicated from the top of the organization to the bottom and, just as importantly, sustained over time.

Although implementation of CPOE should occur as quickly as an organization can take it, the very size of our modern healthcare systems and the complexity of the change required makes this an incremental process. Deciding how big the implementation increments are, and how to ensure, as MMC did, that you "build success upon success" can make all the difference.

Both OSU and MMC demonstrate how success can be achieved by meaningful partnership with industry CPOE leaders, but conversely how "off the shelf" solutions really aren't possible in modern healthcare systems.

Finally, both of these fine organizations demonstrate that significant benefits can and should be realized from the implementation of CPOE, driving the national discussion forward on the imperative to accomplish effective automation in the American healthcare system.

Acknowledgments

Credit for the Maimonides section: The folks who paved the way were:
- Stanley Brezenoff, President - CEO
- Pam Brier, COO

- Samuel Kopel, MD, Medical Director
- Allan Strongwater, MD, Chairman Orthopaedic Surgery & Musculoskeletal Services
- Javier Beltran, MD, Chairman Radiology
- Steven J. Davidson, MD, Chairman Emergency Medicine
- Sondra Olendorf, RN, Sr. VP/Nursing
- Nancy Daurio, RN, Associate VP MIS
- Maxine Fielding, RN, Director Clinical Systems
- Joan Evanzia, RN, Director MIS Training
- Shoshana Haberman, MD, Director Perinatal Testing

References

1. Ahmad A, Teater P, Bentley TD, et al. Key attributes of a successful physician order entry system implementation in a multi-hospital environment. *J Am Med Inform Assoc.* 2002, 9(1):16–24.
2. Anderson JG, Jay SJ, Anderson M, et al: Evaluating the impact of information technology on medication errors: A simulation. *J Am Med Inform Assoc.* 2003, 10(3):292–293.
3. Anderson JG, Jay SJ, Anderson M, et al: Evaluating the capability of information technology to prevent adverse drug events: A computer simulation approach. 2002, *J Am Med Inform Assoc.* 2002, 9(5):479–490.

CHAPTER 5

Designing a Successful Campaign: Leadership Traits

Over the years, it has become clear that despite all chatter to the contrary, there is no way to guarantee success with as large an undertaking as a CPOE/CIS implementation. However, definite character traits and qualities emerge in CPOE leadership that, in retrospect, are more often seen than not. The following construct is an amalgam of the traits seen to be the most common and dominant among those who have contributed to the successful implementation of CIS systems both large and small. As such, they are recommended to the reader for consideration.

AGILITY

Indisputably, the healthcare IT industry has been experiencing change at an amazing rate. Between the rapidly evolving national discourses on errors in medicine, to medical science's advances in information technology, the rate of change has been unprecedented. In this environment, survival—much less success—depends upon one's ability to perceive and respond appropriately to the changing environment. Agility describes this ability to move quickly and easily through these changes. Agility also includes the notion of rapid changing in direction when appropriate to achieve success. This latter characteristic is essential since, to date, no one could claim 100 percent success in anticipating all of the changes in the American healthcare IT environment; hence, errors in judgment and direction are inevitable. The ability to quickly recover from these errors and change course and direction is also included in the notion of agility.

Becoming agile necessitates both a human organizational structure and technological platform designed for such rapid response. Staid vertical organizations, uncoordinated horizontal organizations, as well as the use of immutable technologies, do not foster agility. Without agility, failure is only a matter of time in the current healthcare IT world.

Consider this example. In the last ten years the practice of medicine in America has shifted from provider- and institution-centric to community- and patient-centric. Automation solutions that do not follow the patient and support a continuum of care are obsolete. Similarly, technology has progressed from large mainframes to client server systems and now to the World Wide Web with a general expectation of ubiquitous access to information. Without agility, a physician leader would progressively lose the *hearts and minds* of his/her organization by lagging behind these rapidly changing trends.

PLASTICITY

One of the most profound discoveries in neurology in the past decade is the revelation that the human brain remains pliant and adaptable throughout a lifetime.[1] The most important aspect of this pliancy is the incredibly rich switching network of connections our brains possess enabling everything from remembering the words to a favorite tune to performing delicate surgical procedures. Making new connections is therefore natural for our brains and, as research has shown, the more we use a particular connection, the better it functions. Compare your ability to remember your way to work on Monday morning versus sitting down and playing that piano recital piece that so impressed your parents when you were 12 years old!

Plasticity in the current context applies to your ability to reroute strategies, change tactics, reassign team members, and make all of the necessary changes in a project that may be veering off in the wrong direction, before serious difficulties arise. Plasticity also is the key skill responsible for connecting synergistic groups together to benefit the goals of a healthcare IT effort. For example, physician and nurse groups that work particularly well in the pre-automation environment more than likely have worked out the necessary skills to help one another with new changes, such as the introduction of information technology. Making people in this group the key architects of the physician-nurse educational IT program would be an inspired example of plasticity allowing well-lubricated connecting groups to lead others to success.

An additional notion of plasticity, that frequent use of a particular pathway leads to improved functioning over time, also serves in our context when considering IT team building. One of the best-kept secrets of successful IT implementation is continuous project pilots. Pilot programs allow low risk, low visibility "mini-implementations" to be performed. These achieve a host of goals: (1) program testing and debugging; (2) implementation team process testing and refinement; and (3) mini-competitions allowing those not in the pilot to view glimpses of the system and to become engaged, in the next pilot, out of interest or simply curiosity. Frequent and numerous pilots, therefore, allow the refinement of plasticity for both your organization and its users as well as your IT team.

Consider this example. Because of the multi-year nature of PCIS projects, systems being implemented or developed for healthcare automation are heterogeneous amalgams of technologies and designs. Plasticity of the leadership ensures that the key *connections* between the oldest and the newest aspects of a PCIS project are maintained, and furthermore that when a new component provides enhanced value for an organization, the switch is made.

An example of such plasticity is the notion of a clinical data repository (CDR). A CDR is common data repository of clinical information for the entire PCIS system. This is a totally different construct than the proprietary, system-specific databases of systems of yesteryear. Rather than inpatient databases and outpatient databases, the CDR is the technologic equivalent of the continuum of care clinical strategy allowing information to be patient centric rather than location centric. Plasticity allows the leadership to recognize the strategic value in transitioning from the older database construct to this important new CDR approach thereby enhancing the value of even the earliest components of an organization's PCIS throughout the enterprise.

PERSEVERANCE

Of all of the characteristics of IT leadership, or indeed most successful human endeavors, none is more important than perseverance. It is a fact that from inception to completion, healthcare IT projects require years to complete even in relative small clinical settings. The number of projects that collapse in the first one or two years is unknown, but it is clearly the majority of cases. Beyond vision, beyond creativity, beyond even political acumen, perseverance is an absolute requirement to achieve the full implementation and success of healthcare IT systems. Perseverance remains such an important aspect of IT leadership because most healthcare IT projects are never really over. Even in implementations that succeed the first time out (a microscopic minority of cases), this is the case. One reason is that healthcare IT projects pass through a number of stages:

1. Envisioning;
2. Designing;
3. Building;
4. Testing;
5. Piloting;
6. Disseminating;
7. Evaluating;
8. Maintaining;
9. Upgrading; and
10. Integrating.

Yes, by the time you're "done" implementing your new shiny super system there will be, as certain as tomorrow's sunrise, a new technology, a new business need, an unhappy user group ... just something that will necessitate a significant change to the system making this essentially a never-ending process.

One response to this reality is depression. Another is a sense of job security. But one thing for sure, it takes perseverance to continue to step up to the challenge of this process and succeed.

BELIEF

Over the trials, tribulations, and time it takes to achieve success with healthcare IT projects, one of the key elements, just like in the rest of life, we humans need belief. It might be easier if your project is called a patient care information system rather than a nurses' or doctors' system; however, the same applies. If we are to move forward in the establishment of desperately needed systems to support healthcare in this country, a belief that these systems are important, worthwhile, and possibly even lifesaving is essential. Another reason for including belief among the top characteristics of a successful healthcare IT leader is, especially at academic institutions, the mistaken assumption that if only the "definitive article" on the value of implementation of CPOE, then it would make it so much easier for everyone. This assumption is bad for two reasons: First, there will never be the definitive article in this field (there are precious few in any field), and second, once (if) it was ever written, everyone would lay down their arms and work together—a completely unrealistic expectation, in our opinion.

Implementation of important healthcare IT systems, the successful ones, are all "one-offs." They look, feel, and work particularly for that organization. If you've seem one CPOE installation, you've seen one! Therefore we are left with the reality that there is no definitive proof—economic, technical or other. Arguably, it is belief that leads to some of the most important decisions in our lives, selection of career, choice of spouse, decision to have children, and so forth. So far from being a debit, it is precisely because a leap of faith, or "getting it" in the parlance of the day, is necessary that this field is so interesting.

References

1. Restak R. *Mozart's Brain and the Fighter Pilot: Unleashing Your Brain's Potential.* New York: Three Rivers Press, 2002.

CHAPTER 6

Getting Over It: Hitchhiker's Guide to the Physician-Computer Conundrum

The physician-computer conundrum is a dynamic balance. It is a balance between all of the positive forces leading toward success in implementation of information technology into a healthcare setting as opposed to all of the impediments to that goal. In this book we have endeavored to describe why, over ten years after our first look at the phenomenon of the physician-computer connection, more has not been accomplished. One thing is perfectly clear: There is no magic, never-fail formula for achieving success in achieving the connection. It is also clear that progress towards the goal, although slow, has been made within very different settings around the country and around the world. Nevertheless, the pursuit of the key factors needed to achieve success goes on.

It is now obvious that the key factors are not exclusively techno-logical, behavioral, or organizational, but a combination of all of these, and more. Recent reviews of successful U.S. sites, however, allow us to create a balance sheet of factors that reliably move an organization either toward success or failure in the journey towards what is known

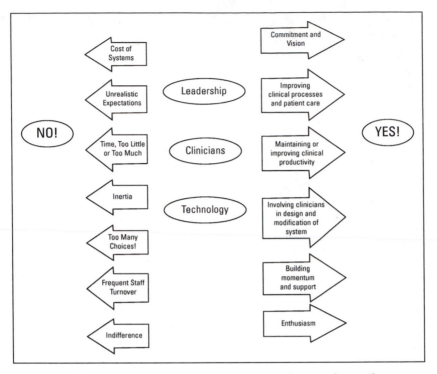

Figure 6-1. The Physician-Computer Conundrum Balance Sheet.

as the physician-computer connection (Figure 6-1). Understanding these factors should lead to a better understanding of which elements of the physician-computer connection can be worked towards and planned, and which are out of the control of mere mortals (see the section on Zen and the physician-computer conundrum, below).[1]

POSITIVE FACTORS

Let us first examine the positive factors directing an organization toward success. Commitment and vision are reliable predictors and essential qualities of successful individuals and organizations. Commitment implies that they are in it for the long haul. As we discussed in Chapter 2, CPOE/CPR projects are multiyear, often multimillion dollar endeavors with significant risk politically. Without the vision to see leadership, clinicians, and an organization through the challenges, CPR/CPOE projects fail, on a regular basis. The converse situations of unrealistic expectations and organizations with frequent staff turnover (unfortunately all too common in healthcare today) nearly always spell disaster for projects like CPOE and CPR. Hence commitment and vision of leadership in particular, but in an organization by consensus, are absolute requirements for success.

Improving clinical processes and patient care are success factors that might seem self-evident; however, in today's healthcare financial environment, they are increasingly being scrutinized in support of expensive CPOE/CPR projects. In the past, purely qualitative and anecdotal justification of the improvements in patient care that occurred with the implementation of CPR systems was sufficient. Now, however, quality studies actually measuring the benefits to patient care of systems are being required for both cost justification (return on investment) as well as marketing to clinicians the justification for the need to change their practices to maximize the value of systems. It should be noted parenthetically that although a body of literature is finally emerging that compellingly demonstrates the value of CPR/CPOE systems, the expertise to craft—much less carry out—such studies is still limited to a select few organizations around the country. Certainly the IT consulting community has begun to rise to this challenge, hopefully enabling the real measurement of value of clinical systems.

Maintaining or improving clinical productivity provides one of the greatest challenges to the leadership of the successful CPOE/CPR project, again especially in the modern era of healthcare economics. It should be stated from the outset, however, that this factor can and is often counter-balanced by perceived value (i.e., improvement in clinical processes and patient care), making this factor a relative one rather than absolute requirement.

Nonetheless, statements such as "If this system takes me more time to order than this pen and paper, I won't use it!" are still heard on a regular basis. There is no question that without "the vision thing" and studies documenting the benefits of moving forward with information technology in healthcare, we will debate the value of technology endlessly. The fact that productivity can be improved is finally being demonstrated by studies that examine the total process of healthcare workflows rather than piecemeal parts. For example, in a recent study of order entry in an ambulatory care environment, there was no significant difference between time spent in the process of patient care between a manual and automated order entry workflow taking into account the entire process in the clinic.[2] With this information, plus post-implementation, locally-collected data, the challenge of maintaining or improving productivity post-automation is being met.

Involving clinicians in design and modification of the system is a factor that was the entire focus of our first book, *The Physician-Computer Connection*. Suffice it to say that although there are many factors that need to be considered before undertaking extensive modification of commercial systems (e.g., cost, time, enshrining bad work flows) there must be meaningful involvement of those who are expected to use CPOE and CPR systems in the configuration and design of these systems. Errors at either extreme (e.g., "Slam in the vanilla system!" or "Make all the changes you want!") will spell costly disaster to even the most well funded and resourceful organizations.

Although building momentum and support are essential for acceptance of the change involved with a clinical information system, these factors require finesse and pacing. That is, if too much enthusiasm is raised too soon, it is guaranteed that both your organization and your staff will be worn out by the time you turn on the switch to go live. Furthermore, if enthusiasm is built upon unrealistic expectations, the backlash from staff and faculty have been strong enough in the past to completely destroy more than one CPR project, the dreaded deinstallation. The notion of a momentum and support plan that builds to a crescendo and reaches its maximum close to the time of system activation seems to work best while avoiding these pitfalls.

Enthusiasm is infectious and one of the most important factors and friends of the CPR/CPOE project. Although visionary leadership can instill it in large groups of individuals, it is each and every individual's job to identify exactly what stimulates their enthusiasm about CPOE/CPR projects. However, this is more than asking "what's in it for me?" Individuals must have both the time and training to understand enough about your project so that they can identify, refine, and formulate exactly what makes them enthusiastic about this project.

Although the majority of your organization's rank and file does not have to be enthusiastic about a project for you to be successful, the right people do have to share this enthusiasm lest you lose the day. Although it is easy to identify the need for the CEO, CIO, and so forth to have enthusiasm towards the project, there is also an informal leadership within all groups (clinicians, allied health, and so forth) that should be identified early and given some special attention, education, and understanding to enable their enthusiasm to grow and become infectious to others. Identifying this influential, but informally identified group is usually quite easy: Just ask anyone in that group who is the person whose opinions sway those of the rest.

Finally, there is the need, especially in large CPOE/CPR projects, for alignment. Alignment is the notion of the physical and temporal convergence of the necessary elements essential to the success of your project. That is, if you have a visionary, committed leader for your project, but he/she leaves your organization years before the project is completed, you obviously have a major risk (if not a guarantee) of failure. Another example: if the planned "go live" of your project happens to have the misfortune of falling during a financial crisis at your organization (e.g., downsizing), once again, you have a high probability of failure. Hence, although we have discussed at length the strategies, preparations, and elements of working toward a successful implementation of clinical information systems, there are undoubtedly aspects of alignment that are completely and totally out of the hands of any mortal. For this reason, and the mental health of the anxious reader, we need to close with the Zen of the physician-computer conundrum.

Zen and the Physician-Computer Conundrum

After thousands of conversations, publications, conferences, how-to books, and so forth, it is clear that there is absolutely no foolproof method of either making or buying a CPOE system and successfully installing it. To be sure, there have appeared characteristics of successful systems, leaders, and organizations, but even when these are all accounted for, there remains the element of alignment as mentioned above. Alignment of organizational culture, of financial status of institutions, of disposition of faculty and staff that would need to go through the change of implementing a CPOE, that simply *must* be in place for the final success to be achieved. This alignment occurs at a pace indigenous to the entities themselves. That is, some organizations are fast moving and hard-hitting, while others take 20 years to adopt electricity. So it is with groups of people. It is in trying to align these large entities that logic and "scientific" efforts fall apart. They are going to move change and be ready for change at their own pace and that's that.

You can make significant and wonderful progress over the time it takes to wait for this alignment. There is much wisdom in the notion that the journey is the reward. Certainly, if you adopt and embrace this Zen-like notion of CPOE direction, you may avoid significant stress-related health and emotional disorders, not to mention live longer in the business.

"What?" you may ask us, "after all these anecdotes, free-ranging advice constructs, and examples, you're saying there is no answer to the conundrum?" No, readers; the answer requires both preparation and patience. Be prepared with the education, training, discussion, and components of success that you've read about in this book and elsewhere. Be patient, for patience is the final key that you hopefully will have—and the insight and peace of mind to recognize that, as with many things, no matter what you do, you cannot change, accelerate, nor, happily, stop them. By all means follow the guidance of Winston Churchill that we repeat below, and "never give up." But likewise understand that there is much to be gained and done in the interval between inception of your vision and its happy achievement. Enjoy the journey, embrace the chaos of human interactions and affairs, and never, never, never, never give up.

Success to date has almost always been a happy mistake. The most compulsive efforts to analyze the critical elements of success for a CPOE have, to date, essentially shown that success or failure is best related to alignment. Let's face it, folks, this journey called Life is a relatively short one. The alignment of most elements is entirely out of the control of any one person, even the most powerful and elite of leaders. Success, however, often falls to those individuals with the perspicacity to notice when alignment of the critical factors for CPOE success occurs, who then—and only then—press the charge toward completion of the project.

In conclusion, after carefully avoiding all of the pitfalls mentioned in this text, and garnering all the key advantages needed for success, the ultimate outcome of success or failure will depend, as all great events do, on chance. Fear not, embrace the chaos of life and strive on, as it may well be the struggle towards your goal that is the greatest gift of all.

"Never give in.

Never, never, never, never,

in nothing great or small, large or petty,

never give in except to convictions of honor and good sense.

Never yield to force; never yield to the apparently overwhelming might of the enemy."

—*Sir Winston Churchill*

References

1. Doolan DE, Bates DW, et al. The use of computers for clinical care: a case series of advanced U.S. sites. *J Am Med Inform Assoc.* 2003, 10:94–107.

2. Overhage JM, Perkins S, et al. Controlled trial of direct physician order entry. *J Am Med Inform Assoc.* 2001, 8:361–371.

Hitchhiker's Guide to Careers for Physicians in Applied Medical Informatics

One of the reasons the physician-computer conundrum exists is due to the need for more physicians to commit to careers in the IT industry. Ideally, these physicians act as translators between the technical and clinical worlds, thereby enabling better systems, better integration of technology into patient care workflows, and improvement in outcomes that matter, e.g., reduction in errors in care delivery. It has been a privilege to be a member of this rapidly evolving world of applied medical informatics over the past 20 years, prompting this appendix in which we describe: (1) what are the major categories of careers for clinicians in healthcare IT; (2) what skill sets are needed to be successful in each role; and (3) observations on the significant changes in opportunities for physicians over the past few years.

At the top level, there appear to be three fundamental career paths that physicians have taken in the industry. They include careers with vendors, consulting companies, and provider organizations.

Before we examine these career paths, though, we need to make a plea for the following: (1) go to school! (2) get meaningful experience *relevant* to the career path you've chosen—don't assume that all healthcare IT roles and careers all operate the same; and (3) network!

Regarding the latter point of networking, as physicians we are deeply affected by role models in our careers. Although role models in physician healthcare IT careers are a bit harder to find, they are out there! There are numerous organizations where you can discuss, probe, and learn from the experience of others in moving down the path to career choice in healthcare IT.

Regarding the necessity for education and relevant experience, over the years, far too many clinicians have jumped directly from medical school or immediately post-residency into healthcare IT roles. In the past, on-the-job-training may have been a reasonable place to start because there were few models of physician IT careers and most traditional MPH and MBA programs were not geared to preparing physicians as leaders in healthcare IT. Times have changed. There are now many excellent degree-granting programs actually tailored for physicians interested in approaching healthcare IT careers. It is still important to select the *correct* post-grad training to aid in your career (see below); however, it is probably no longer adequate to jump in from residency and intuit the skills you'll need for a successful career.

Failure to obtain the proper educational preparation can lead to unnecessary frustration and disappointment for several reasons: (1) vendors, consultants *and* provider organizations are looking for intervals with experience as the single most important differentiating characteristic. Experience obviously takes time, and both salary and position will be lower if you enter a company at the introductory level; (2) experience tempers and refines your selection of career choice. That is, after experiencing initial leadership in a CPOE or other CIS project, you learn what you enjoy about the role and get a notion of what would not be interesting; and (3) experience aids in informing you of what you don't know. This may directly lead to other educational opportunities that significantly change your life, options, and career.

Now we return to the three main career options for physicians in applied medical informatics.

Vendor: Sales "Demo Doc," Marketing (Medical Trendreader), R&D- Doc Programmer or Programmer Doc. One of the oldest career tracks for physicians in healthcare IT is the "join the vendor" path. Although the excitement and logic of following this path may be intuitive, there are many pitfalls that the young clinician should be aware of. First, amazing as it may seem, vendors are in business to make money! Although interest in new development and vision to improve the quality of healthcare in America are part of every company's stated goals, the reality of "no money, no mission" is sometimes a very hard one to learn for many young clinicians. Compare the language of margins, quarterly profits, and share prices with the young hopeful's desire to "Make a real difference", bring the real clinical story to the vendor world, or make systems that physicians will really want to use. Worse, far too many clinicians apply for vendor positions with far too little preparation and experience as we discussed previously.

Consultant: Enthusiastic Newcomer, Seasoned Senior Physician, Xmen-Public Health/Policy, business and other industry leaders who just "happen" to be MDs.

Physicians in IT consulting business take on an entirely different paradigm. The product is you, or at least the firm that you are representing. Although lack of experience, true authoritativeness, and credibility can be clouded with company "indoctrination" and orientation, most customers can identify the inexperienced junior rep a mile away and, more importantly, since costly consultation time is sought primarily to inject experience and credibility into an organization, the engagements are usually sought with senior consultants. Without personal experience and credibility, consultation experience reads like a "canned lecture" from a drug company.

Therefore it is necessary to come to consulting IT careers with several upfront expectations: (1) you are already experienced in the healthcare IT field and have a wealth of that experience to share; (2) you have an existing reputation in the field and are an asset to your company as such; (3) you love to travel, a lot. Did we mention that you have to *love* to travel, a lot? There is no getting around the reality that physician consultants may be "on the road" five or six days out of the week. Although this might be attractive to the young carefree physician, this lifestyle takes its toll on anyone after a while.

Provider: CMIO, CPOE/CIS/CPR project MD leaders, CMO/Department Chair "enlightened physician leader."

The most common, and in many ways the best, way for physicians to embark on healthcare IT careers is through hospital/health system IT roles. These usually take the form of participation in CPR/CPOE clinician project committee work. Although valuable, there are several important differentiating points the physician who wishes to pursue a career in IT should be aware of. These are

1. Leadership in IT projects;
2. Perspective;
3. Reporting relationships; and
4. Presentation and publication.

Although everyone must start somewhere, it is extremely important that the physician anticipating a career in healthcare IT seek a recognized, meaningful IT leadership role within projects. We use the term "recognized" because it is only through organizational recognition and promotion that you will be able to gain both the necessary experience as well as identification as a leader in your hospital/health system and build the initial resumé necessary for future opportunities. Meaningful leadership means that indeed there are clearly defined aspects of your IT project that you are in charge of and others will be looking to you for the answers.

The reporting relationship for the physician in a provider organization anticipating an IT career is important for several reasons. First, you need to gain understanding and experience in communicating with the top leadership of IT administration. This is important both from an opportunity standpoint (i.e., some physicians decide that becoming a CIO is their ultimate goal) as well as effectiveness (i.e., for many aspects of provider organization IT projects, there is an essential and ideally complementary interplay between physician lead and CIO, that is necessary for the success of medium to large projects).

The reporting relationship is also important for the credibility of the physician leader. If fellow clinicians identify you as the person who speaks directly with the CIO and has the power/authority to make things happen through that association, you will be sought after and recognized as a key asset of the medical staff. Just as important, if the physician lead reports directly to the CIO, there will be opportunity for enhanced administrative and business insights and networking that can also significantly affect your ability to achieve your career goals.

Finally, your reporting relationship can build lasting industry relationships and network connections that open doors and opportunities that a purely clinical approach to healthcare IT leadership cannot. For example, although there are a wealth of clinical IT organizations (such as AMIA and AMDIS), there are many more healthcare CIO/business organizations (e.g., HIMSS) providing key experience, employment, and networking opportunities to aid you in your career.

Presentation and publication are essential to building a successful career in healthcare IT for the simple reason that you won't be hired if no one has ever heard your name! Although the number of publications and opportunities were severely limited in the early days, now there are venues galore for everything from peer reviewed scientific informatics publication (e.g., *Journal of the Applied Medical Informatics Association*) to breezy but well-read industry journals. Naive physician beware: do not ignore the latter category. Many, many people important to the industry read these publications regularly and although the articles may not bear the clinical gold standards of prospective randomized controlled studies, they are nonetheless often quoted and will provide an excellent way for you to break into the national scene with significant credibility.

A new and important publication venue has arisen in the World Wide Web. Although first generation Web IT publications had variable quality, there are now some truly excellent, well-read healthcare IT-specific Web publications that also provide a rapid entree to the new healthcare IT career-bound physician to express his/her thoughts and gain recognition (see www.informatics-review.com, www.imia.org, and www.himss.org).

Presentations naturally stem from provider organization IT leadership ("how we did it" lectures) to national IT strategy symposia and think tanks. Although there has been some contraction in the healthcare IT meeting agenda in the past few years (post 9/11), there remain abundant opportunities for local, regional and national healthcare IT presentations. Avail yourself of these as they are appropriate to your goals. That is, if your trajectory is toward the academic side, be sure to be a regular contributor to the AMIA national meetings. If more inclined to the business side of healthcare IT, the HIMSS national meeting is currently the *must see and be seen* meeting. In sum, it is key to craft a regular and natural connection between your work and achievements in your institution and your communication of those achievements nationally both in publication and presentations.

In addition to the above categories there are a host of other potential career opportunities for the physician in healthcare IT: These include (1) business entrepreneurship; (2) healthcare policy and legislation thought leaders; and (3) informatics program developers and educators, as well as many others. In general these career paths are less traveled and tend to be pursuits that occur as byproducts of careers in the previously mentioned major categories.

In sum, the opportunities available and potentially available in healthcare IT for physicians is truly limitless in the new millennium. With the pervasiveness of information technology in our lives and work, these distinctions may be as tightly integrated into medicine as they are becoming in other industries. The excitement lies in the fact that those adventurous souls who take the risk of pursing these careers today will be on the front lines of shaping that future. Go get it!

Acronyms

ALOS	average length of stay
AMA	American Medical Association
AMDIS	Association of Medical Directors of Information Systems
AMIA	American Medical Informatics Association
CDR	clinical data repository
CEO	chief executive officer
CIO	chief information officer
CMIO	chief medical information officer
COO	chief operating officer
CPOE	computerized provider order entry
CPR	computerized patient records
CPRS	computer-based patient record systems
DSS	decision support system
EHR	electronic health records
EMR	electronic medical records
FTP	file transfer protocol

HIMSS	Healthcare Information and Management Systems Society
HL7	Health Level Seven
IOM	Institute of Medicine
LDS	Latter-Day Saints Hospital
MACS	Maimonides Access Clinical System
MCIT	medical center information technology
MI	myocardial infarction
MMC	Maimonides Medical Center
NHS	National Health System (Great Britain)
NLM	National Library of Medicine
OSU	Ohio State University
PACS	picture archiving and communications systems
PC	personal computer
PDA	personal digital assistant
PCIS	patient care information system
RRIS	results reporting information system
UMHHS	University of Michigan Hospitals and Health Systems
VA	Department of Veterans Affairs (former Veterans Administration)

Index